Tuva Publishing
www.tuvapublishing.com

Address Merkez Mah. Cavusbasi Cad. No:71
Cekmekoy - Istanbul 34782 / Turkey
Tel: +9 0216 642 62 62

Rainy Day Sewing

First Print 2019 / July

All Global Copyrights Belong To
Tuva Tekstil ve Yayıncılık Ltd.

Content Sewing

Editor in Chief Ayhan DEMİRPEHLİVAN
Project Editor Kader DEMİRPEHLİVAN
Designers Amy SINIBALDI, Kristyne CZEPURYK
Technical Editors Leyla ARAS, Büşra ESER
Graphic Designers Ömer ALP, Abdullah BAYRAKÇI, Zilal ÖNEL
Photograph Amy SINIBALDI, Kristyne CZEPURYK
Illustrations Amy SINIBALDI, Kristyne CZEPURYK

ISBN 978-605-9192-16-3

CONTENTS

PROJECTS

INTRODUCTION

Rainy day sewing is the best, don't you think? Stay in your pajamas, drink tea, eat soup, throw on an old favorite movie… and sew days. Those are my fave. So we've compiled here a book filled with fun and easy sewing projects perfect for those days - or any day - rain or shine! But before we get sewing, I'd like to share a story with you.

I've told many stories over and over - about how I got my first sewing machine on a whim on Father's Day at Target, and how I named nanaCompany after my family's first names initials - but I'm going to share a really special and fun story with you now. That is, how I met my first sewing friend. At the time, I literally knew no one in real life who liked to sew and buy fabric. It was just me, my machine, and a growing number of online "friends" who form our amazing supportive global sewing community. It was 2011. I'd recently begun blogging. And out of the blue one day, Kristyne of Pretty by Hand wrote me and said, "Hey I'm going to be in California this summer. Let's get together."

Of course I was a little nervous but I said yes. And I've met hundreds of sewing friends since - in real life. But there will always be something special about my friendship with Kristyne and it's more than just the long phone calls, the belly laughs and support and shared experiences over these last eight years. There is a crystal clear memory in my head and heart from that first day we met.

I remember where we were (in little Tokyo in Los Angeles) and what we were looking at (cute stationery) and how we dared say out loud to one another, though it was more of a hushed whisper, "Wouldn't it be so cool if one day we were fabric designers??" Of course, it was nothing more than a pipe dream at the time - we never actually thought it would happen. But here we are today. We are both fabric designers. Both book authors. Pattern designers. And now, like putting a cherry on top of a rich and fabulous sundae… we've accomplished writing a book together.
Truly a dream come true.

Of course I couldn't have asked for a better friend/coauthor. Kristyne has seriously impressive skills in areas where I may be lacking and her sewing ability, as you know, is nothing less than perfect. Made it very easy to work together. And I feel that we've both brought something unique to the table, yet our styles mesh well together. It isn't the first time we've collaborated creatively. Likely not our last. I hope you enjoy this book and have many wonderful any day sewing moments!

xx Amy

Kindred Spirits: "two people that make a special connection through a shared interest." That's what Amy is to me. I found her almost a decade ago, when I discovered the wonderful online world of blogs and Flickr, and I fell instantly in love with her beautiful makes and photography. There was something different … special … indefinable about her style. She had a way of combining fabrics, notions, colours and details that filled my soul with pure joy.

Coincidentally, we started blogging within a month of each other, way back in early 2011. It was happenstance that I found myself in her corner of the world (we lived 1,570 miles apart) that summer. I took a chance and invited her to meet me for "coffee", something rather out of character for me.
It turned into the most wonderful afternoon. I'll always remember how kind, and sweet, and fun she was - exactly as one would expect based on her creations. We giggled, and laughed, and talked a lot. But my strongest memory is of us standing in a little Japanese bookstore, daring to say our dreams out loud about what we wanted to accomplish in this global community of quilters we'd found ourselves in. Our bucket lists were remarkably similar: monetize our blogs (check!), see our work published in magazines (check!), sell patterns (check!), write a book (check!), and the wildest dream of all was to design fabric (check!). The final dream that took the longest for us to accomplish - not for lack of trying - was to write a book together. Well … check, here it is!

Amy and I spent endless hours of fun creating these projects for you. My favourite moments while writing this book - other than all the laughing we always seemed to do - were talking through project decisions with her. She could start to describe an idea and I understood exactly where she was going before she finished a sentence. Or I could ask her for advice and she never failed to come up with a brilliant suggestion within seconds. She's the best creative dance partner. I'm in awe of her talent, and I'm so grateful to call her friend.

Kristyne ♡

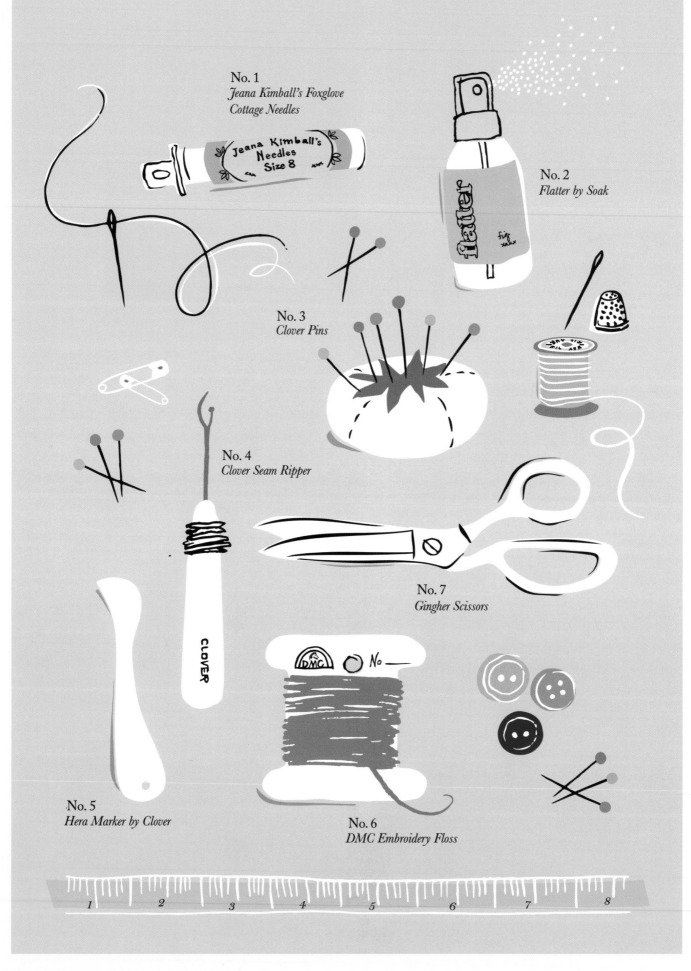

No. 1
*Jeana Kimball's Foxglove
Cottage Needles*

No. 2
Flatter by Soak

No. 3
Clover Pins

No. 4
Clover Seam Ripper

No. 7
Gingher Scissors

No. 5
Hera Marker by Clover

No. 6
DMC Embroidery Floss

TOOLS OF THE TRADE

» **SELF-HEALING CUTTING MAT**
An essential tool when cutting fabrics with a rotary blade cutter. Do yourself a favor and get the largest mat you can fit in your workspace, as quilting fabric runs around 42" wide and it's easier if you can make the cut in one single roll with your rotary blade.

» **OLFA ROTARY CUTTER WITH ENDURANCE BLADE**
We both started our quilting adventures by cutting fabrics with scissors (a tedious task), and when we got our rotary cutters we never looked back. It is an invaluable tool and we highly recommend the Olfa Endurance Blades for sharpness, precision, and less strain when cutting fabrics.

» **NON-SLIP QUILTING RULERS**
Transparent, non-slip, acrylic quilting rulers used with the rotary cutter and self-healing cutting mat make cutting multiple layers of fabric a breeze. But most importantly, the quilting rulers (which come in many shapes and sizes) allow for accurate cutting. When ⅛" of an inch can make a sewing project go askew, accuracy is key and these rulers are a must-have.

» **GINGHER SCISSORS**
High quality tools make any job easier and although there are many excellent choices for scissors, Gingher is a classic that has stood the test the time because they are a superior scissor. We also love spring-loaded thread snips and a smaller pair of embroidery scissors for the sewing room.

» **TAPE MEASURE**
A long tape measure is flexible, longer in length than any quilting ruler, and is super convenient for quick measuring on the fly.

» **JEANA KIMBALL'S FOXGLOVE COTTAGE NEEDLES**
There are so many needles to choose from. Amy always chooses whatever is one sale, but Kristyne's go-to brand is Foxglove Cottage. Whether you're appliqueing, hand-quilting, embroidering, or simply doing some general hand sewing, Foxglove has the right needle in your favourite size.

» **FRIXION ERASABLE PEN**
Sometimes you need to mark fabric for things like embroidery or button placement. We've grown to rely on FriXion pens for these tasks. They come in a variety of colours, the marks are easy to see, but they WILL disappear with heat. (Note that the marks will reappear when exposed to very cold temperatures, but a hot iron will fix that in a jiffy!)

» **CLOVER SEAM RIPPER**
A good seam ripper is every sewist's worst best friend -a necessary evil. But let's face it. Mistakes happen. And for the both of us, the choice is clear: if a sewing mistake is bothersome (and you can't hide it with an embellishment), rip those stitches out and sew it again.

» **HERA MARKER FROM CLOVER**
For marking without ink, the Hera marker is a wonderful tool we use again and again. Not only is it convenient for marking sewing lines, but quilting lines as well.

» **GLUE STICK**
Amy uses a glue stick, Kristyne not so much. It is very useful for temporarily holding pieces in place while sewing them together and can take the place of pins when pins may be too cumbersome.

» **FUSIBLE WEB**
If you've never used it, we warn you that invisible, double-sided adhesive is a bit weird. And you must follow the manufacturer's instructions or you'll end up with a sticky mess on your iron. Cautions aside, we love using it to position two objects together with perfect accuracy an without pins! We use it for everything from machine applique to labels, to basting lace trim.

» **505 TEMPORARY FABRIC ADHESIVE**
Obviously, pins are a must-have for sewists. But sometimes they get in the way or cause minor distortions on smaller projects. (Or if you're like us, you live on the edge and run right over them with your sewing machine needle, tsk tsk!) 505 spray adhesive is formulated specially for sewing so we like to use it for basting small, layered projects like pot holders, tote bags, and mini quilts. A little goes a long way and it won't gum up your needle!

» **FLATTER BY SOAK**
This wonderful starch-free smoothing spray relaxes wrinkles in your fabric (even the tough crease from being folded on the bolt or in your stash for a while), helps your patchwork lay flatter, and leaves it smelling fabulous! It's also environmentally friendly, and is gentle for sensitive skin.

» **CLOVER PINS**
We've talked about straight pins much more than we'd ever dreamed, and the verdict was clear: We both love Clover pins. And pinning. Again for accuracy and precision.

NOTES

» WHERE TO BUY FABRICS?

We both have very sizable stashes of fabric to work with and yet that never keeps us from stopping into a local quilt shop where ever one is found to look for more cute fabric. So to answer the question of where do we buy fabric - the answer is anywhere cute fabric can be found. Of course we do have a few favorite online shops and Sunny Day Supply (sunnydayfabric.com) consistently carries the cutest fabrics from the US and Japan. Fat Quarter Shop (fatquartershop.com) is a larger shop carrying the latest fabric collections, tools and books. And an endless supply of tools, fabrics, and trims can always be found at Etsy by doing a simple search for the item in mind (for example: a search for printed cotton ribbon will bring up a treasure trove of cute cotton labels from which to choose).

» TO WASH OR NOT TO WASH?

Both Amy and Kristyne prefer not to pre-wash their fabrics after careful consideration of trying both methods (washing, and not washing). No discernible difference was found that made taking the extra step of pre-washing a pre-requisite for best results. If anything at all, the preferable choice is to work with nice crisp fabrics as the fabric was received. And as they both work with high quality cotton fabrics, color bleeding is not often a concern but a color catcher thrown in the wash is always a good idea for that first wash and if red fabrics have been used.

» NOTES ON PRESSING

It cannot be stressed enough that pressing pieced fabric with a hot iron should be exactly what the term implies: pressing. Putting pressure on the seam from above and not pushing the iron back and forth, which may distort the seam or fabric shape. Adding a spritz of Flatter starch-free spray will further improve pressing results (and make your sewing space smell heavenly!). As for seams, it is always preferable to press seams towards the darker fabric if possible. Pressing seams open is appropriate if the patchwork is small, or there is too much bulk at a seam, while pressing to one side is preferable when seams can be nested. Which is all to say that how you press your seams can vary by project and fabric placement and there is no categorical wrong or right, but rather what seems to work best at each particular seam -which is entirely up to you!

» NOTES ON CUTTING

Consistency is key. If you cut fabrics to the left of the marking line, the right of the marking line, or dead center, please do it consistently every time. Shoot for accuracy. We're human, we get it. But accuracy in sewing is important, otherwise we wouldn't make patterns that include information down to the ⅛". When you feel unsure, slow down! Slowing down is so much more than an act, it is a state of mind, which tends to lead to better results. And above all, please carefully replace dull rotary cutter blades the moment you are straining to cut through fabrics. You'll thank yourself immediately.

Seam allowances should all be ¼" unless otherwise specified. For instance, when turning an item with curves, a less than ¼" seam allowance may be preferable (the mouse and cat). Corners may be clipped in order to reduce bulk when turning an item right side out, but stitches should always be left intact.

TECHNIQUES

» PINNING

The use of pins (or, if preferred, long basting stitches) is highly recommended for matching seams when sewing patchwork. It is a step that may be overlooked but I think you'll find that much better results are achieved if ample pinning is used when sewing two or more layers of fabric together.

» THE QUILT SANDWICH

The quilt sandwich is composed of three layers. The bottom layer is the backing, which is laid with the wrong side up. Tape the edges to the work surface to keep the backing smooth and straight, but not too taut. Next, a piece of cotton batting, fusible fleece, or other batting is placed on top. The patchwork is placed on top, right side up. So the quilt sandwich always has a fluffy center and the three layers must be quilted in order to keep them all together in one place.

» BASTING

Before quilting any project, basting is necessary. This keeps the three layers of the quilt sandwich in place and prevents shifting. The amount and type of basting necessary depends on the size of the patchwork piece you are quilting. For small pieces, basting spray may be all you need, along with perhaps a few pins. If it is larger than 20" I recommend using long basting stitches or rust-proof safety pins spaced about 4" apart, beginning at the center and radiating out.

» QUILTING

The process of quilting always involves a needle and thread, which passes through all three layers of the quilt sandwich. Quilting may be ornate or utilitarian, very dense or sparse, depending on the maker's desired look. Quilting methods include stitching or tying by hand, sewing by sewing machine, or sewing by a specialty long-arm machine.

» 1. HAND QUILTING

Quilting by hand is a lovely time-consuming process that involves making dashed lines of stitches and creates a soft look and feel to the quilted piece. Amy has always liked to use DMC Perle Cotton No. 8 or No. 12 in Ecru for hand-stitching. The stitches are made using a rocking motion with a longer quilting needle and a dashed line is the result. A quilting hoop is helpful for larger quilts but is not necessary for smaller pieces. If you're new to hand-quilting, do try this technique on a smaller quilted piece to see if you enjoy the process. We do.

» 2. TIED QUILTING

Using a sturdy thread, tie a "square knot" at even intervals throughout. You can tie the knot on top of the quilt or on the backside, and then trim tails so that they are equally long - about 1" in length. The space between knots depends on the type of batting used and the manufacture instructions will include minimum space requirements between knots. This method of quilting would be charming on the doll quilt as it creates a very authentic vintage look.

» 3. QUILTING WITH A SEWING MACHINE

Simple straight-line quilting on a domestic sewing machine with a good walking foot is another enjoyable way to quilt. Ample pinning of the quilt sandwich is necessary for this technique. The amount of lines (for example horizontal lines at ½" apart or lines sewn at angles) can create wildly different looks and varied denseness in a quilt. Again, experiment with this. Try moving the fabric rhythmically while stitching to create wavy lines (one of Amy's favorite techniques).

» 4. FREE MOTION QUILTING

This is a slightly more advanced technique on a domestic sewing machine using a darning foot. The feed dogs (the sewing machine "teeth" that normally guide fabric through the machine) must be lowered so that the quilt sandwich can be moved freely. Then, the motion of the fabric through the machine - and by consequence, the pattern of stitches on the quilt - is controlled entirely by you. It takes a lot of practice to find your groove and to learn to stitch smooth even lines but practice definitely makes perfect and (again) small pieces are perfect for experimenting. Non-slip quilting gloves are a must-have as they help to get a good grip on your fabric and control the movement. Slow and easy is a good pace when free-motion quilting.

» 5. LONG ARM QUILTING

This method of quilting is often called "sending it out" unless you yourself own, or have access to, a long arm machine. Services can generally be easily found and the results can be gorgeous. The drawbacks may be the cost of the service and the feeling that the handmade item is no longer fully one's own. Amy and Kristyne love the look of professional long arm quilting especially on larger quilts or quilts that may be enhanced by intricate quilting design work.

BINDING

» HOW TO MAKE BINDING

1 Lay two fabric strips right sides together at a 90° angle with the ends extended about ½". Pin and sew a seam from inside corner to inside corner as shown.

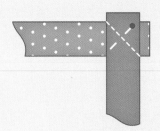

2 Trim the corner seal allowance to ¼" and press seam open.

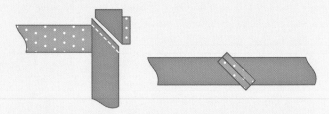

3 Repeat until you have the desired length. Then press the binding in half lengthwise, wrong sides together.

» HOW TO SEW BINDING TO A QUILT

1 Place one end of the binding in the middle of the quilt bottom edge, align raw edges, and leave a 6" tail of the binding. Pin and sew a ¼" seam. When you get to the corner, stop ¼" in from the edge with the sewing machine needle down. Sew a few back stitches and remove the quilt from the machine.

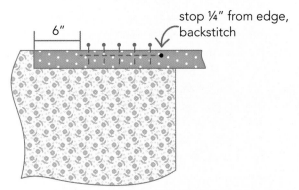

stop ¼" from edge, backstitch

6"

2 Turn the quilt 90° so the next edge is on the right. Flip the binding upwards and away from the quilt with a 45° fold. Pin the fold.

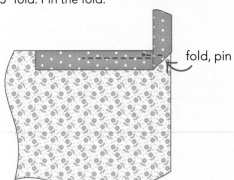

fold, pin

3 Fold the binding down laying the raw edge of the binding along the raw edge of the quilt. Start sewing from the top edge of the quilt, and repeat steps 2-3 until you are 12" away from where you started stitching.

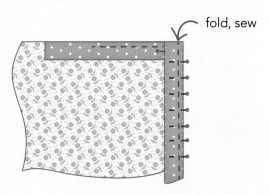

fold, sew

4 Remove the quilt from the machine. Lay the binding tails along the edge fo the quilt until they meet in the middle of the 12" space. Then trim the tails to measure 2" extra from the point where they meet.

trim tails to 2" from where they meet

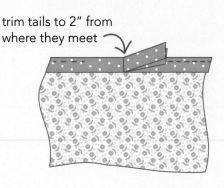

5 Join the ends with a mitered seam like you did when you made the binding. Trim the seam allowance to ¼", and press open. Refold the binding in half and finish sewing it to the quilt. Then fold the binding over to cover the raw quilt edges and hand stitch in place on the back.

PROJECTS

ANTON
CRO

ART. NO. C4636/3 COLOR

Spotlight Cushion

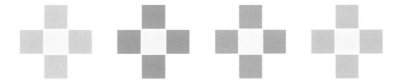

I'm not kidding at all ~ the Spotlight cushion is going to be your new best friend. It takes no time to make, uses up only a teensy amount of those fabrics you want to showcase, you'll turn to it again and again (so easy-going!), it's supportive (it's got your back), and... it's just plain lovely. Simple in design yet quietly sophisticated. Liberty and linen for the background are an obvious choice, but denim and any of your favorite prints would also be fabulous.

SIZE
21" x 12 ½"

» 4 charm squares (5" x 5") of assorted cotton prints

» ½ yard of linen

» ⅓ yard muslin or plain fabric for lining

» ⅓ yard batting or fusible fleece

» 22" x 13" cushion filler

CUTTING

» Sixteen 1¾" squares of assorted prints - four squares for each "spotlight" block

» Twenty 1¾" squares of linen

» Five 1¾" x 4¼" rectangles of linen for between the "spotlights"

» Two 21¾" x 5" rectangles of linen for the top and bottom borders

» One 23" x 14" rectangle of quilting for the patchwork lining

» One 23" x 14" rectangle of batting or fusible fleece

» One 8" x 13" rectangle of linen for the envelope style back

» One 19" x 13" rectangle of linen for the envelope style back

INSTRUCTIONS

1 To make a spotlight block, sew 4 matching prints and 5 linen 1¾" squares together into a 9-patch. Press all seams towards the spotlight fabric. Make 3 more blocks.

2 Sew five rectangles of background linen 1¾" x 4¼" at the ends and between each spotlight. Press all seams open.

3 Sew the two linen rectangles (21¾" x 5") to the top and bottom sides fo the patchwork. Press seams open.

4 Make a quilt sandwich using batting or fusible fleece and the lining rectangle (23" x 14"). Quilt as desired.

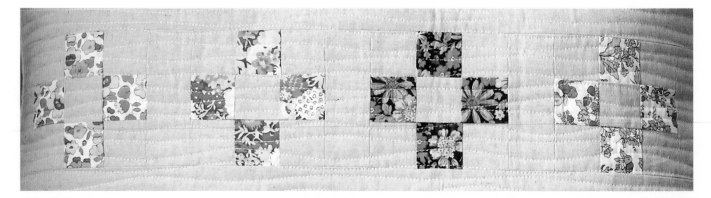

5 To make the envelope back, finish the end of the 19" envelope backing piece of linen by pressing a ½" fold of fabric at short edge of fabric. Fold the raw edge of fabric in another ½" and top-stitch. Repeat with the 13" piece of envelope backing linen.

6 With right sides together, pin the short piece of envelope backing aligned to the right side of the cushion.

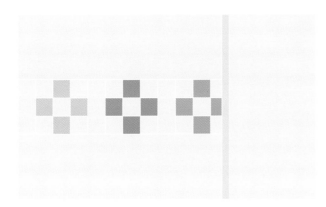

7 With right sides together, pin the long piece of envelope backing on top, aligned to left side of cushion. It will overlap the short piece of backing by approximately 3".

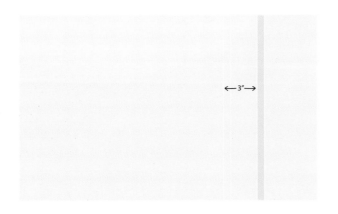

8 Sew around the 4 edges completely and finish the unfinished edges with a zig-zag stitch.

9 Turn cushion right side out through envelope opening. Ease out corners gently. Press well.

10 Insert filler into the cushion.

Rain Drops
Potholder

Raindrops Potholder

I don't really think there is anything more appropriate than making a Raindrops Potholder on a lovely drizzly morning. When you're finished, bake a plate of cookies, make a pot of tea, and pat yourself on the back. That's my kind of morning!

As usual, I wanted to highlight some very special fabrics for this project and in this case they are original feedsack prints from the 1930's. The very kind of prints that have been the inspiration behind thousands of 30's repro designs that fabric lovers know and love today. I have a friend named Sam, who is a NICU nurse and an intrepid feedsack hunter. She has always found the cutest authentic feedsack prints and I have been lucky enough to be someone she has shared them with. Don't they look so charming in this potholder?

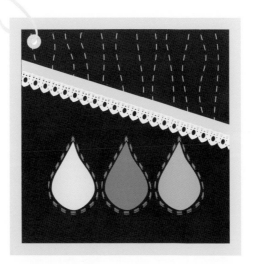

SIZE
9" x 9"

» 1 FQ of black linen

» 3 cotton print scraps, at least 3" x 4"

» 1 FQ contrast print for binding

» 10" length of crochet trim, approx ⅓" wide

» 1 F8 double-sided fusible web

» 1 F8 insulated batting

» Water soluble glue stick

» One eyelet, approx ½"

» 10" length of string or ribbon for hanging loop

CUTTING

» Four 9 ½" squares of black linen

» Three 2" x 3 ⅛" rectangles of various feedsack scraps

» One 9 ½" length of crochet trim

» One 54" length of binding

INSTRUCTIONS

1 For the back of the potholder, make a sandwich with one piece of black linen right side down, then the insulated batting, then one square of fusible fleece, and finally one piece of black linen right side up. Baste all four layers together and quilt as desired. Trim to measure a 9" square. Set aside.

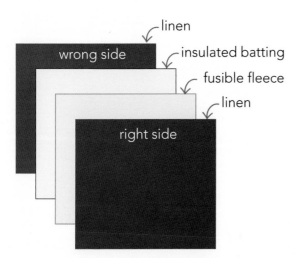

2 To begin the front of the potholder, trace the rain drop template onto the paper side of the fusible web.

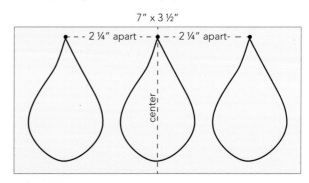

3 Following the manufacturer's instructions, adhere the fusible web to the wrong side of one 9 ½" square of black linen, centered with the bottom edge of the fusible web 1 ½" above the bottom edge of linen. With the fusible web paper is still on the linen, very carefully make a snip in the center of each raindrop, and continue to cut the three raindrops out. Then gently remove the paper backing.

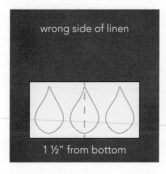

4 To add the raindrop fabrics, dab a glue stick around the outermost edges on the right side of a raindrop rectangle. Press it quickly to the wrong side of your black linen with raindrop cut-outs so that it fills the cut-out completely. Repeat until all three raindrop cut-outs are filled. Smooth with your fingertips.

wrong side of linen

5 Next, make another quilt sandwith with a black linen square facing wrong side up, then the fusible fleece with the fusible side upand then the raindrop panel, right side up. Take care to keep the raindrop fabrics in place. Press with your iron to set. Machine-stitch roughly (free-motion, if you like) around the raw edges of your raindrops several times to secure.

6 Trim the raindrops panel to measure 9" square. Then mark a dot at 1" down from the upper left hand side and 4" down from the upper right hand side. Trim a diagonal line from one mark to the other.

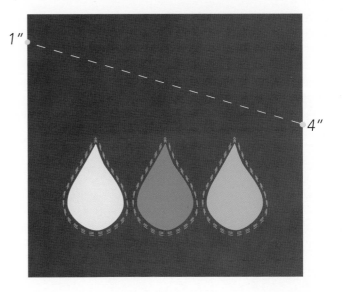

1"

4"

7 Add binding and crochet trip to angled top edge.

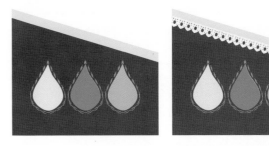

8 Lay the potholder front on top of potholder back, aligned at bottom edge. Pin well and zigzag stitch around all four sides. Add binding.

9 Following the manufacturer's instructions, attach an eyelet to upper left corner of the potholder. Then thread a ribbon or string through the eyelet for hanging.

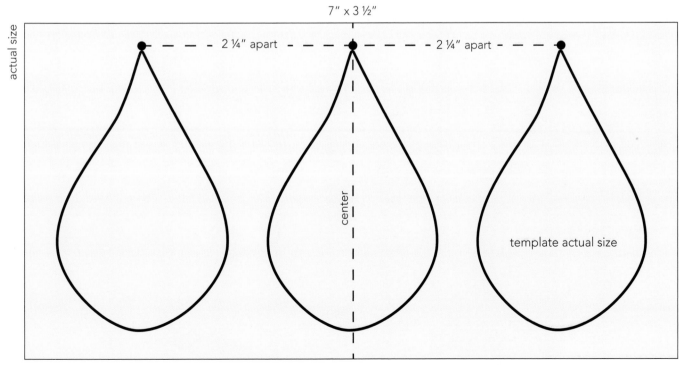

7" x 3 ½"

2 ¼" apart   2 ¼" apart

actual size

center

template actual size

Johnny Appleseed Quilt

Johnny Appleseed Quilt

Apple motifs have always been a favorite of mine. Well thanks to this lap-sized quilt, which is perfect for every season, you'll get your fill of apples all year long! There is only one block in this simple modern design: the apple block, and it's really quite simple to sew. Chain piecing will allow you to complete the top in a weekend but maybe you'll prefer to sew up just an apple a day? Have fun choosing colors for this quilt and don't be afraid to think outside the box. For this version I stayed traditional with pinks and greens but I do love the idea of a rainbow of apples!

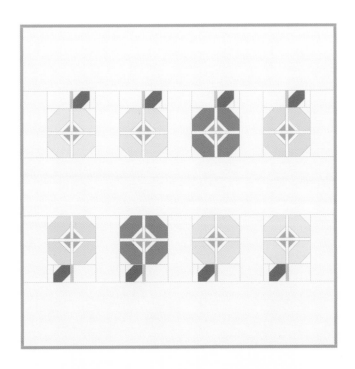

SIZE
56" x 56"

» 3½ yards background fabric

» 32 charm squares - in sets of 4 - of assorted prints for apples 1

» F8 brown fabric for seeds

» 1 F8 light green fabric for stems 1 F8 dark green fabric for leaves

» ½ yard contrast print for binding 4 yards backing

» 62" x 62" piece of quilt batting

» Marking pen, such as a FriXion pen

CUTTING

» *From Seeds Fabric*
(A) Thirty-two 1 ¾" squares

» *From Assorted Apple Fabrics*
(C) Thirty-two 4 ½" squares 7 (4 squares for each apple)

» *From Leaf Fabric*
(F) Eight 3 ½" squares

» *From Stem Fabric*
(I) Eight 1" x 3 ½" rectangles

» *From Background Fabric*
(B) Sixty-four 2 ½" squares for blocks
(D) Sixteen 1" x 4 ½" rectangles for blocks
(E) Eight 9" x 1" rectangles for blocks
(G) Sixteen 2" squares (for leaves)
(H) Eight 4 ½" x 3 ½" rectangles (for leaf/stem)
(J) Eight 1 ½" x 3 ½" rectangles (for leaf/stem)
(K) Ten 4 ¾" x 12" rectangles (sashing between apples)
(L) One 56" x 10 ½" rectangle (middle sash)
(M) Two 56" x 11 ½" rectangles (outer sashes)

» *From Binding Fabric*
Five 2" x WOF strips

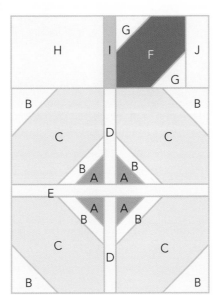

1 For one apple block, place an A square onto a B square, aligned at the corner. Using a fabric marker, draw a diagonal line through A square and stitch on the line. Trim the outer corner, leaving a ¼" seam allowance. Press the seam open. Make four units.

Make 4

2 Lay the seed unit on a C square, right sides together, aligned at corner. Draw a diagonal line through seed unit, as shown, and stitch on the line. Trim the outer corner, leaving a ¼" seam allowance and press the seam open. Make four units.

Make 4

3 Lay B square on the opposite corner of one apple unit, right sides together. Draw a diagonal line through white square, and stitch on the line. Trim the outer corner, leaving a ¼" seam allowance and press the seam open. Make four units.

Make 4

4 Sew two apples units to a D rectangle. Press seams toward background fabric. Repeat with remaining two apple units.

Make 2

5 Sew the two apple units to an E rectangle. Press seams toward background fabric.

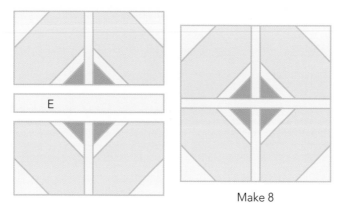

Make 8

6 To make a leaf unit, lay two G squares on opposite corners of an F square. Draw diagonal lines through the G squares, and stitch on the lines. Trim the outer corners, leaving a ¼" seam allowance. Press seams open. Then add a J rectangle to the right side of the leaf. Make 8 leaf units.

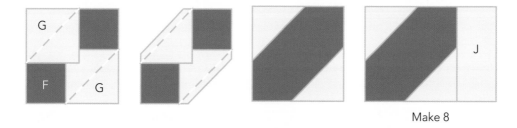

Make 8

7 To make a stem unit, sew an H and I rectangle together. Press seam open.

Make 8

8 Join a stem and leaf unit. Press seam open. Make 8 of these units.

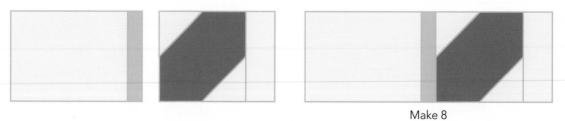

Make 8

9   Sew the stem + leaf unit to the apple unit. I suggest pinning where the stem and center of apple meet so that they are aligned. Make 8 blocks.

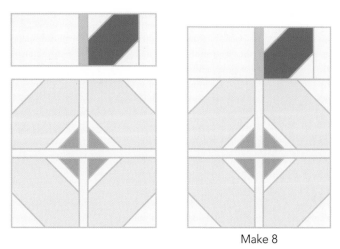

Make 8

10   To make one row, sew 4 apple blocks and 5 K rectangles together. Press towards the background rectangles. Make 2 rows.

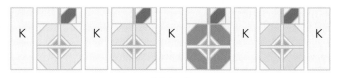

Make 2

11   To assemble the quilt, sew the two rows, L rectangle and two M rectangles together. Press towards the large background rectangles.

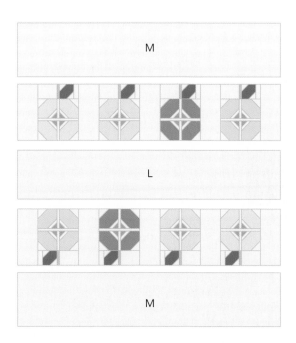

12   Assemble the quilt sandwich. Layer the backing right side down, batting, and quilt top, right side up. Baste and quilt as desired (I quilted straight lines at a cross-hatch, 1 ½" apart). Trim and bind.

Gifted Bag

Gifted Bag

This bag alone is quite a gift on its own, but if you put a little something inside it's really special. The construction of this gift bag is my favorite. Deceptively simple and fun to make, the key to a nice crisp structure is pressing at all the sides. The grommet details and ribbon handles add a familiar finishing touch. Just add a fat quarter as "tissue paper" and your gift-wrapping is complete!

SIZE
8" x 9" x 3"

» ½ yard of cotton print for bag ½ yard of cotton print for lining

» FQ contrast cotton print for binding

» F8 brown fabric for seeds

» Grommet kit (½" size grommets) with 4 grommets 1 yard of rope or ribbon

» ½ yard of SF-101 Shape-Flex by Pellon or other fusible interfacing

CUTTING

» One 21 ½" x 12" rectangle of cotton print for bag exterior

» One 21 ½" x 12" rectangle of cotton print for bag interior

» Two 11 ½" x 1 ½" strips of fabric for binding

» Two 21 ½" x 12" rectangles of Pellon SF-101 Shape-Flex woven fusible interfacing

INSTRUCTIONS

1 Using the manufacturer's instructions, press one piece of SF-101 woven fusible interfacing to the wrong side of the 21 ½" x 12" rectangle of bag fabric. Trim to measure 21" x 11 ½".

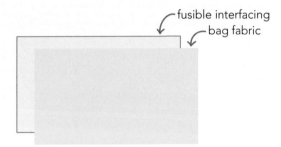

fusible interfacing
bag fabric

2 Lay one binding strip along a short end of the bag rectangle, right sides together. Sew it in place. Add the second strip to the other 11 ½" end of bag exterior. Press the binding strips towards the seam allowance.

3 Fold the interfaced bag exterior in half, wrong sides together. Press the fold well to form a crease. While folded in half, open one side and measure a fold of 1 ½". Press the crease. Flip over, and repeat on other side. Press well.

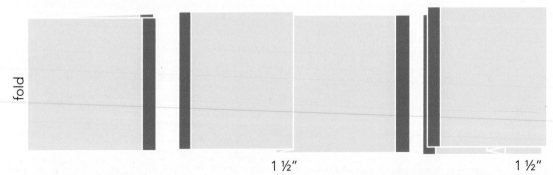

fold

1 ½"   1 ½"

4 With right sides together, maintain the "M" fold at the bottom of the bag and keep the binding up (not folded over the bag edge). Sew the sides together, adding a few extra back-stitching at both ends of the seam.

5 Turn bag right side out. Press the side seams open. Press creases into all sides of the bag to give it a crisp shape. Fold the binding down against the outside of the bag to expose the seam created when it was attached to the bag.

6 Repeat steps 1-5 with the lining fabric and interfacing EXCEPT omit the binding and keep the lining inside out.

7 Insert the lining into the bag and ease it into place. Pin and baste the top edges of the bag and lining together, with a scant ½" seam, making sure to align the side seams.

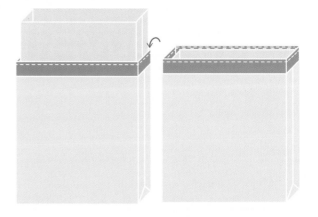

8 Fold the binding upwardalong the seam. Then fold the unfinished binding edge towards interior of bag, ⅜" and press. Press the fold again another ⅜".Make sure the binding looks even on inside and outside of bag. Use a glue stick, pins, or clips to keep the binding in place while you top-stitch in the ditch between binding and bag to catch the binding on inside of bag. Optional: stitch by hand, or machine stitch ⅛" from the bottom edge of binding.

9 Following the manufacturer's instructions, install 2 grommets 4" apart and centered on the front and back sides (approximately 1" from top edge). Thread the ends of ribbon or rope through the grommets, and tie knots at each end on the inside of bag.

Sidewalk Quilt

Sidewalk Quilt

When designing this quilt, my mind was off on an adventure, wandering city blocks and sidewalks, skittering down secret alleys. The result was surprisingly simple and sweet and I immediately recalculated the quilt to make it a baby quilt. I like it in soft colors but I can see it just as fabulous in bolder colors to accentuate the graphic elements. If you need to make a quick baby quilt for someone special, this sweetly modern design will surely come in handy!

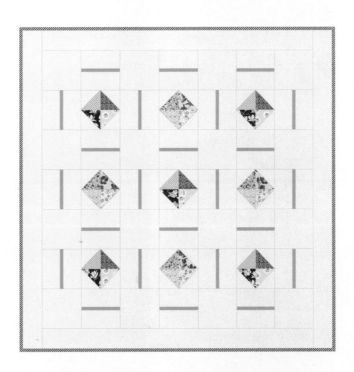

SIZE
48" x 48"

» 3 charm squares each of 4 assorted blue prints for a total of 12 squares

» 2 charm squares each of 4 assorted pink prints for a total of 8 squares

» 2 ¼ yards "sweet macademia" solid fabric for background

» ⅛ yard "toasty walnut" solid fabric for "sidewalk" bars

» 2 ½ yards backing

» ½ yard contrast fabric for binding

» 54" x 54" batting

» Marking pen, such as a FriXion pen

CUTTING

» *From Assorted Charm Squares*
Twenty 4 ¼" squares

» *From Contrast "Sidewalk" Fabric*
Four 1" x WOF strips

» *From Background Fabric*
Twenty 4 ¼" squares
Sixteen 6 ½" squares
Eight 3 ¼" x WOF strips
Two 42 ½" x 3 ½" rectangles (horizontal borders)
Two 48 ½" x 3 ½" rectangles (vertical borders)

» *From Binding Fabric*
Five 2" x WOF strips

INSTRUCTIONS

This quilt has one block design in two colours. Each block has 4 different prints.

5 x    4 x

1 Each block is made of 4 half-square triangles (HSTs). To make and HST, lay one 4 ½" print square and one 4 ½" background square right sides together. Draw a diagonal line on the wrong side of the background square. Sew ¼" on both sides of the line. Then cut along the line. Press the HST units open. Trim to 3 ½" HST units. Repeat until you have 5 HSTs of each blue print and 4 HSTs of each pink print for a total of 36 HSTs. (You will have 2 extra of each blue print.)

2 To make a block, chose one HST of each print from the same colour. Sew them together, pressing seams open. Make 5 blue blocks and 4 pink blocks.

5 x   4 x   5 x   4 x

3 To make the sidewalk sashing, sew two 3 ¼" x WOF background strips together with one 1" x WOF sidewalk strip. Make 4 of these units.

4 x

4 Subcut each strip into 6 ½" units for a total of 24 pieced 6 ½" squares.

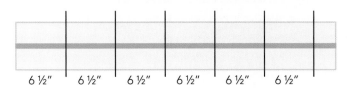

6 ½"   6 ½"   6 ½"   6 ½"   6 ½"   6 ½"

5 Make for of these rows with alternating sidewalk sashing squares and solid background 6 ½" squares.

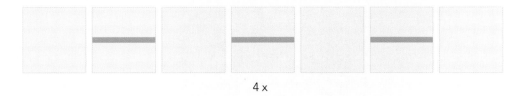

4 x

6 Make the following three rows with alternating sidewalk sashing squares and pieced blocks.

2 x

1 x

7 Sew the rows together.

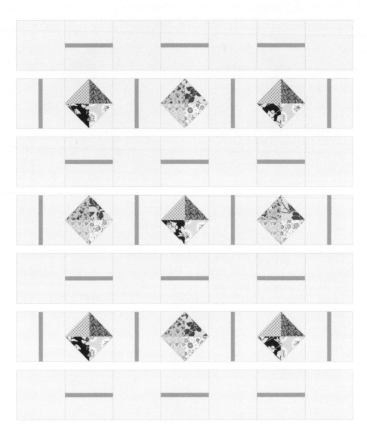

8 Attach the two 42 ½" x 3 ½" borders to the top and bottom of the pieced quilt top. Press seams open. Then sew the 48 ½" borders to the sides. Press seams open.

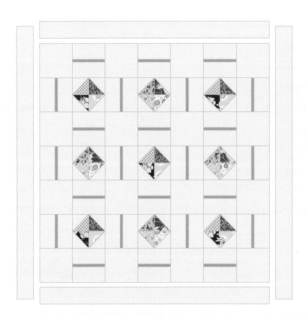

9 Assemble the quilt sandwich. Layer the backing right side down, batting, and quilt top, right side up. Baste and quilt as desired. Trim and bind.

Playtime Tuffet

Playtime Tuffet

I imagine this playtime tuffet being used for tea parties, but of course it's also useful as extra seating for family gatherings or friendly company. The practical yet decorative handle makes this soft home accessory perfect for toting around the house for a toddler's lounging or as a cozy cushion. The simple design on the top is simple and fun, but you can use your imagination and treat it as a blank canvas for your favourite patchwork, orphan blocks, or pretty applique.

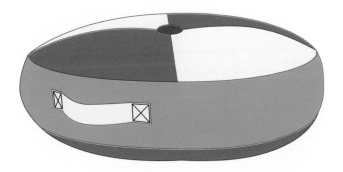

SIZE
18 ½" x 18 ½" x 4"

» 4 Fat Quarters of assorted cotton fabrics for top

» ⅓ yard of contrast fabric for sides

» ⅔ yard of fabric for bottom

» 1 Fat Eighth fabric for handle

» 1 yard cotton batting

» 1 large bag of polyester stuffing

» 2 self-covering buttons, approx 1 ¼" diameter (plus assembly tools)

» 2 fabric squares, of contrast prints for top and bottom buttons

» Extra long needle

» Button thread

» Large piece of cardboard or a few sheets of regular paper + tape

» String and pencil (to trace circle)

····················· CUTTING ·····················

» *From Assorted Top Prints*
Four squares 11" x 11"

» *From Contrast Fabric*
Two strips 4 ½" x WOF

» *From Bottom Print*
One square 22" x 22"

» *From Handle Fabric*
One strip 3 ½" x 9"

» *From Batting*
Two squares 22" x 22" for top and bottom
One rectangle 4 ½" x 60"
One rectangle 1 ¼" x 8" for handle

····················· INSTRUCTIONS ·····················

1 To make the cushion top, sew the 4 squares together. Press seams open. Lay the patchwork right side up onto a batting square. Pin or baste the layers together, and quilt as desired.

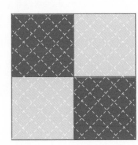

2 To make the cushion bottom, lay the bottom fabric square right side up onto one batting square. Pin or baste the layers together, and quilt as desired.

3 To make a circle template, use a piece of cardboard that is at least 20" x 20", or tape sheets of paper together to make a square that size. Cut a 25" length of string. Tie one end of the string to the pencil. Measure 9 ½" along the string, starting from the tip of the pencil and insert a pin at that mark. Position the pin in the center of the paper or cardboard square. Hold the pencil with the string taut and draw a circle. The circle should meaure 19" across. Adjust the string and re-draw if necessary. Cut out the circle.

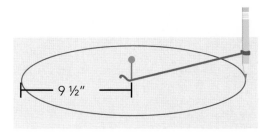
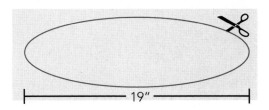

4 Using the circle template, cut out both the quilted top and bottom into circles.

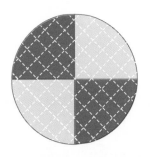

5 To make the handle, fold and press the fabric rectangle in half lengthwise. Open the fold and lay the batting strip along the pressed line. Fold and press the fabric over the batting as shown so all the raw edges are secured inside. Sew along the edges, making sure to sew through all layers. The finished handle should measure 1 ¼" x 8".

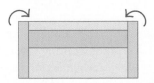
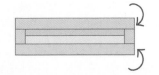

6 To make the side strip, sew the two 4 ½" strips together at the short ends. Press seam open, and cut to measure 60" long. Pin or spray baste the batting to the wrong side of the fabric strip, and quilt as desired. Trim the strip to measure 58 ¾" long.

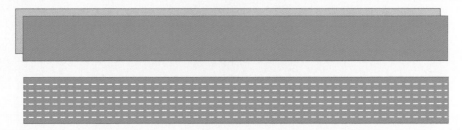

7 Find the approximate center of the strip and mark with a pin. To determine the position of the handle, use pins to mark a 7 ½" span at the center mark, and then remove the center pin. Align one handle end to one 7 ½" mark, and pin the handle in place. Align the other handle end to the other pin that is 7 ½" away. Sew the ends to the strip as shown, adding an X inside a square to help reinforce the handle.

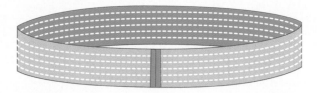

7 ½"

8 To finish the strip, pin and sew the short ends together to form a circle. Press seam open.

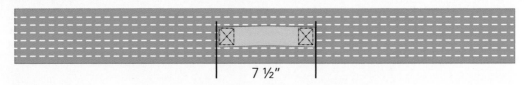

9 Fold the top circle in half and mark the folds with pins. Open and refold in the opposite direction, mark folds with pins. Use the same method to find and mark the four center points for the sides strip. With right sides together, pin the sides strip to the top, matching the pins. Sew the two pieces together. Repeat with the bottom circle, leave a 6" opening.

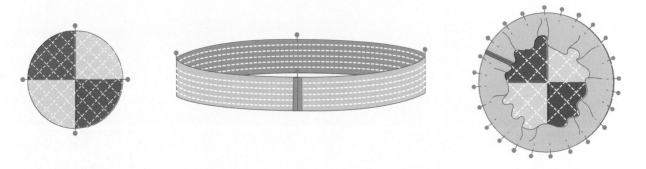

10 Turn the cushion right side out. Fill with stuffing to desired density and hand sew the opening closed.

11 Following the manufacturer's instructions, make two self-covered buttons. Using an extra-long needle and strong button thread, sew both buttons to the center of the cushion to form a tuft.

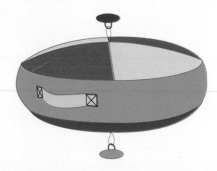

Fabric Button Cards

Pretty little things have always been a favorite of mine. These fabric button cards are proof that the simplest of projects can be so satisfying. I could make these all day for a wall display of pretty buttons. The combination of a floral print and a text print, sets the tone. What a pleasure, rummaging through my button stash and making the little arrangments of six buttons for each tag. And what I love about the construction of these button cards is the interfacing that gives them just the right stiffness and body. Make two or twenty button cards ~ go all out! But I bet you can't make just one!

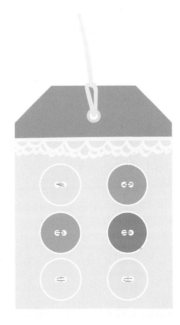

SIZE
3 ¼" x 5"

» 1 charm square of linen

» 2 fabric scraps - floral and text prints, at least 4" x 2"

» 4" x 6" rectangle of fabric for backing

» 4" length of crochet trim

» 4" x 6" rectangle of medium to heavy weight fusible interfacing, I used Pellon 809 Decor Bond

» Button card template

» Water soluble glue stick

» One small eyelet, plus istallation tool

» 10" length of twine or ribbon for hanging loop

··· CUTTING ···

» One 3 ¾" x 1 ¾" rectangle of print for top

» One 3 ¾" x 3 ¾" square of natural linen

» One 3 ¾" x 1" rectangle of text print for bottom

» One 3 ¼" x 5" rectangle of fusible interfacing (Pellon 809 Decor Bond) cut using template

» One 3 ¾" x 5 ½" rectangle of backing fabric

··· INSTRUCTIONS ···

1 To make the card front, sew the three fabrics together with cotton print above linen square and the text print below the linen square. Press seams open.

2 Using the glue stick, baste the crochet trim along the top seam. Stitch in place.

3 Using the tag template, cut the piece of fusible interfacing. Center the interfacing tag to the wrong side of your fabric with the glue side down. Follow the manufacturer's instructins to adhere the fusible interfacing to the fabric. Lay the pieced tag front and the tag backing fabric right sides together. Sew around the edge of the interfacing, leaving a 2" opening on one side for turning.

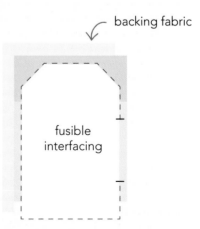

backing fabric

fusible interfacing

4 Trim the corners and edges well. Less than a ¼″ seam in places is expected. Gently turn right side out, easing out all corners. Use the glue stick to press the seam allowance at the opening around the interfacing shape. Sew the opening closed by hand.

5 Following the manufacturer;s instructions, attach a small eyelet to the top center of button card. Use the template as guide for placement. Tie a string or ribbon to the tag.

6 Have fun going through your buttons and pick out an arrangement of six. Sew the buttons to front of card, leaving thread on the back like a traditional button card.

Button Card Template

3 ¼″

5″

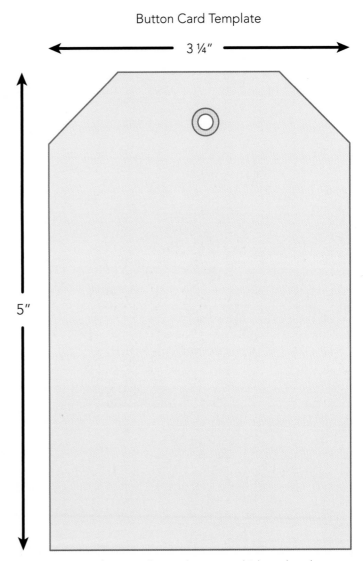

Make a sturdy template using thick cardstock.

Cottage Needlebook

Cottage Needlebook

Pretty notions and tools somehow always seem to make a sewing task more fun. Having equally pretty containers and holders for our supplies ... well, they're just so nice to to see sitting in a sewing box, a drawer, or wherever you keep such things. This little needlebook ticks all the boxes - cute, practical, and fun to make. These cute little cottages make for the perfect gift for all your stitchy friends.

SIZE
2 ½" x 4"

» 1 F8 linen

» 1 FQ of printed fabric

» 1 charm square of felt or wool

» 1 charm square of medium weight fusible interfacing

» 1 charm square of fusible web

» 1 charm square of quilt batting

» 1 skein of embroidery floss

» Square ruler (at least 4" x 4")

» Scalloped scissors or pinking shears (optional)

» Fray Check seam sealant (optional)

» *From Linen*
Two 3" x 4 ¼" rectangles

» *From Printed Fabric*
One 1 ½" x 5 ¼" bias-cut strip for roof
One ¾" x 10" bias-cut strip for bow
One 4" x 2 ½" rectangle for door

» *From Fusible Interfacing*
One 2 ½" x 4 " rectangle for house back
One 3 ½" x 2" rectangle for door

» *From Quilt Batting*
One 2 ½" x 4" rectangle for house front

» *From Felt or Wool*
One 2 ½" x 2 ¼" square

» *From Fusible Web*
One 2 ½" x 2 ¼" square

1 To make the house front, pin or spray-baste the batting to the wrong side of the linen, aligned at the top edge with a ¼" seal allowance on the sides and bottom. Quilt as desired.

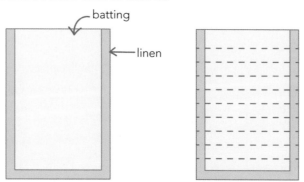

2 To make the house back, fuse the interfacing to the wrong side of the linen, aligned at the top edge with a ¼" seal allowance on the sides and bottom.

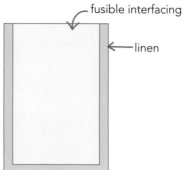

3 Lay the house front and back with right sides together, aligning all sides. Place them on a cutting mat, centered on an obvious line. Place a square ruler on a 45° angle, aligning the corner with the center line on the cutting mat.

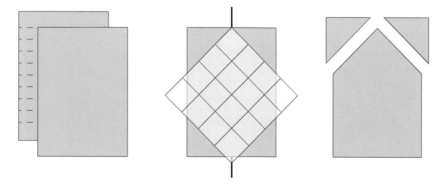

4 Following the manufacturer's instructions, adhere the fusible web to the back side of the felt or wool square. Trim with decorative scissors to measure 1 ½" x 1 ¾". Remove the paper backing.

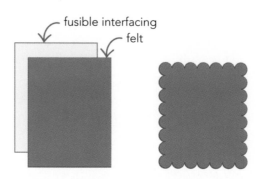

5 To make the door, adhere the fusible interfacing piece to the wrong side of the door fabric rectangle, leaving a ¼" seam allowance on the top, bottom, and a ¾" seam allowance on the sides. With right sides together, fold the door in half as shown. Sew across the top and bottom edges, leaving a 1 ⅜" opening along the side with the wider seam allowance. Sew a few reinforcing stitches at both ends of the opening. Trim the outside corners, and clip the inside seam allowance. Turn the door right side out, gently ease out the corners to make them square, and press. Sew a button to the right side of the door, centered along the edge.

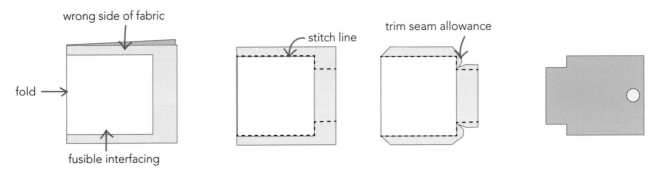

6 To position the door, first lay the felt onto the right side of the house back, aligning it ⅜" from the bottom and centered left to right. Gently slide the door "hinge" under the left side of the felt square, leaving about ⅛" of the hinge visible. Remove the felt and pin the door in place. Stitch down the center of the hinge seam allowance.

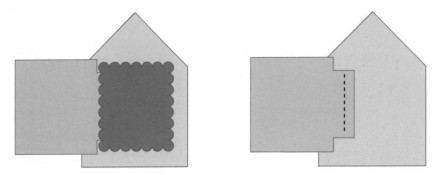

7 To make the buttonhole loop, cut 3 lengths of embroidery wfloss - 10" each - and braid them into a 4" length. Knot both ends to keep the braid intact.

Note: The knots will be cut off after the loop is stitched in place to prevent lumps under the felt.

4" floss braid

8 To position the buttonhole loop, fold the braid in half. Place the felt square back into position, insert the ends of the braid at the center of the right side of the felt, and pin in place. Close the door and test the length of the loop with the button. Adjust as needed, remove the felt, and repin. Sew the braid ends in place, making sure the stitches will be hidden once the felt is installed. Trim away the knots.

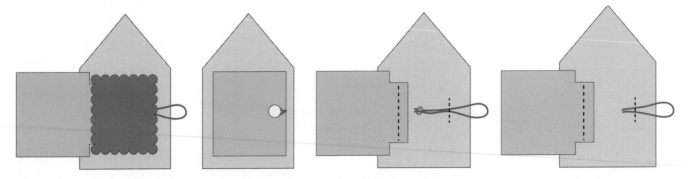

9 With the door open and the loop laying flat, position the felt once more over the door hinge and button loop. Adhere it in place, and top stitch around the edges with a ⅛" seam.

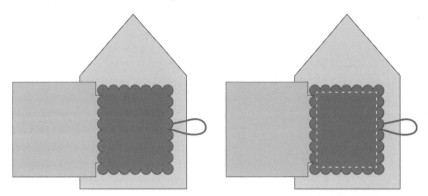

10 Pin and sew the house front and back right sides together down the sides and bottom, leaving the roof edges open. Backstitch at both ends of the seam. Trim the seam allowance at the bottom corners. Turn the house right side out, shape the corners and press.

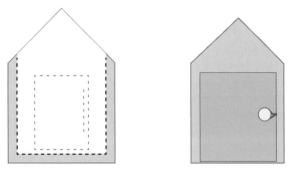

11 To prepare the roof binding, press each short end of the bias strip ¼" wrong sides together. Next, press the strip in half lengthwise wrong sides together. Then open the strip and fold the long ends so the raw edges meet in the middle along the pressed line. Refold in half and press well. Flatter non-spray starch is helpful.

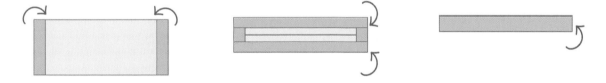

12 Find the center of the roof binding and pin it to the house. Make sure the edge of the house fills the binding . Hand stitch both sides of the binding to the house, and stitch the folded edges of the eaves to each other.

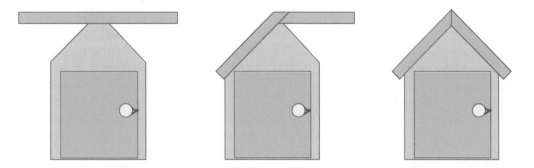

13 To make the fabric bow, repeat step 9 with the bow strip, except do not fold in the short ends. Press very well. Tie the folded strip into a bow. Each loop should be ⅝", and trim each tail to measure 1". Slip stitch any gapes that appear along the folds. If you want, add a dab of Fray Check to the ends. Using the photo as a placement guide, stitch the bow to the house front.

Love You to the Moon and Back Mobile

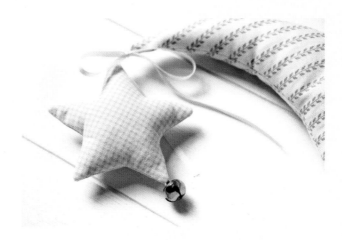

There is a classic children's book you may know as well- about a moon and some socks, among other things- that I loved to read with my kids. That book has never gone out of style and neither will this kid's room decor. It is simplicity at its best. I also like the idea of using gently loved clothing to make the moon and star even more special. The jingle bell adds a sparkly finishing touch!

SIZE
13½" x 13½"

- » ½ yard fabric for moon

- » 2 charm squares for star

- » ½ yard quilt batting

- » 24" length of ribbon for hanger

- » Polyester stuffing

- » Small bell

- » Spray fabric adhesive (optional)

CUTTING

- » *From Moon Fabric*

Two moon shapes with the template (cut one reversed)

- » *From Star Fabric*

Two star shapes with the template (cut one reversed)

- » *From Batting*

Two moon shapes with the template (cut one reversed) - cut at seam allowance line

Two star shapes with the template (cut one reversed) - cut at seam allowance line

- » *From Ribbon*

One 12" length for moon hanger

One 8" length for star hanger

One 2" length for star loop

INSTRUCTIONS

1 To make the moon, pin or spray baste a batting moon to the wrong sides of both moon fabric pieces. To add the hanging loop, fold the 12" ribbon in half and pin the ends as indicated on the template. Sew them in place with a scant ¼" seam.

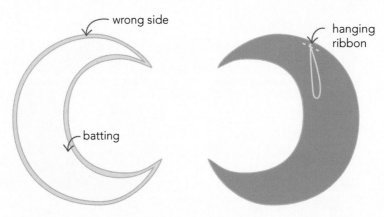

wrong side

hanging ribbon

batting

2 Lay the moon shapes right sides together and pin around the edges. Reduce the sewing machine stitch length to small and sew the pieces together with a ¼" seam, leaving a 3" opening as indicated on the template. Take care to keep the hanging ribbon free inside. Then clip the seam allowance all around the edges. Turn the moon right side out and gently ease the points out. Stuff with polyester batting, and hand-stitch the opening closed. To add the star hanger, fold the 8″ ribbon in half and hand-stitch to the top point.

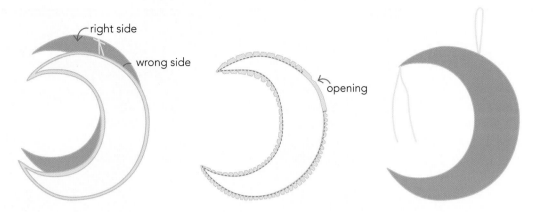

3 To make the star, pin or spray baste a batting star to the wrong sides of both star fabric pieces. To add the hanging loop, fold the 2″ ribbon in half and pin the ends as indicated on the template. Sew them in place with a scant ¼″ seam.

4 Lay the star shapes right sides together and pin around the edges. Keep the sewing machine stitch length small and sew the pieces together with a ¼″ seam, leaving an opening as indicated. Then clip the seam allowance at the inside points and trim all the outside points.

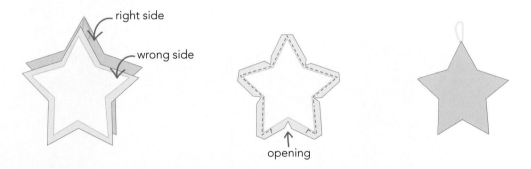

5 Turn the star right side out and gently ease the points out. Stuff with polyester batting, and hand-stitch the opening closed. Then hand stitch the bell to one point,

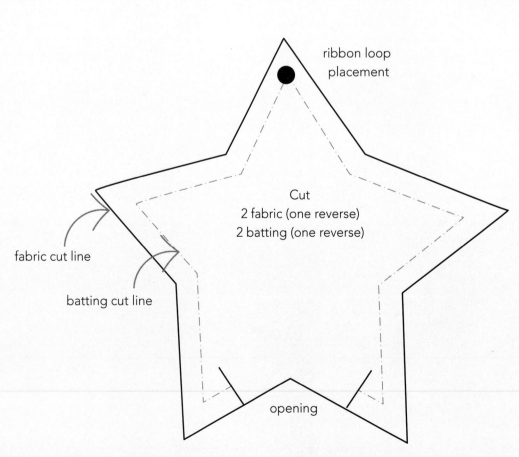

ribbon loop
placement

Cut
2 fabric (one reverse)
2 batting (one reverse)

fabric cut line

batting cut line

opening

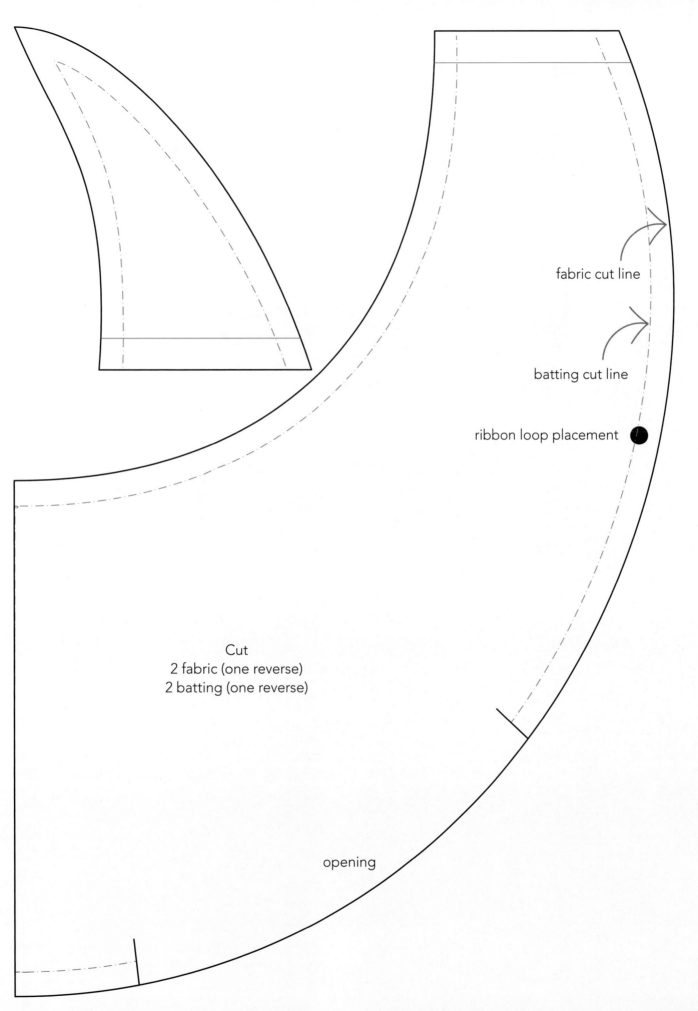

fabric cut line

batting cut line

ribbon loop placement ●

Cut
2 fabric (one reverse)
2 batting (one reverse)

opening

Little Critters Cross Stitch Tote

Little Critters
Cross Stitch Tote

Can you picture a child walking out of the library with this sweet little tote filled with books? I sure can! And anything we can do to encourage our children to read is definitely worth doing. Now, about this simple design ... it really let's all the attention go straight to the adorable row of friendly little critters. I don't know about you but I'm always in the mood to stitch up something

SIZE
9" x 10.5"

» 1 Fat Quarter of taupe Essex linen for bag front and back

» 1 Fat Quarter of contrast print for bottom edge and lining

» 10" length of lace

» 1 Fat Quarter of cotton batting

» 1 pair of purse handles, 12" long

» One skein each of these DMC floss: white, 310, 317, 318, 648, 761, 819, 838, 948, 3713, 3828, 3862, 3863, 3864

» 32ct waste canvas, 3" x 12"

» Embroidery needle

» Embroidery hoop

» Spray fabric adhesive (optional)

» Marking pen, such as a FriXion pen

CUTTING

» *From The Linen*
One 14" x 14" square for bag front
One 9 ½" x 11" rectangle for bag back

» *From The Contrast Fabric*
One 9 ½" x 2" strip for bag front bottom
Two 9 ½" x 11" rectangles for lining

» *From The Batting*
Two 9 ½" x 11" rectangles

INSTRUCTIONS

1 Pin the waste canvas to the linen as shown, 3" above the bottom edge of the linen.

2

Following the pattern, cross stitch the design to the linen. Remove waste canvas if necessary.

DMC Mouliné Stranded Cotton Art. 117				
✕ 838	✕ 317	✕ 3862	✕ 317	✕ 3826
✕ 3863	✕ 318	✕ 318	✕ 819	✕ 948
✕ 948	✕ 3713	✕ 3713	✕ 761	✕ 761
✕ 310	✕ 761	✕ 948	✕ 310	⊠ Blanc
	⊠ Blanc	⊠ Blanc		✕ 310
	✕ 310	✕ 310		

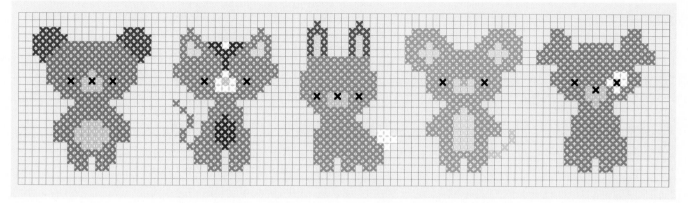

3

Trim the stitched bag front to measure 9 ½" x 9 ½" with the bottom edge of the stitching 1" from the bottom edge of the linen and with ¾" of linen on either side of the stitching.

4

Sew the contrast band to the bottom edge of the bag front. Press seam allowance open. Then sew the lace trim along the seam between the linen and the contrast band.

5

Pin or spray baste the bag front to one batting rectangle, with the right side of the bag facing up. Repeat for the bag back. Using a large spool of thread, trace and cut a curved edge at the bottom corners.

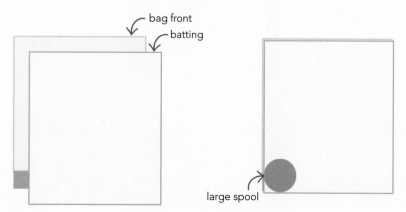

bag front
batting
large spool

6 With right sides together, sew the front and back together along the sides and bottom, rounding the corners as you sew. Trim and clip the corner seam allowance. Turn the bag right side out and press the edges.

7 To make the lining, lay both rectangles right sides together. Trace and cut a curved edge at the bottom corners. Sew the side seams, but leave the top and bottom edges open.

8 With the bag right side out and the lining inside out, slide the bag inside the lining. Pin around the top edge and sew the two pieces together.

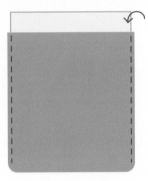 

9 Pull the lining up over the top edge of the bag, but do not insert it into the bag yet.

10 Lay one handle so the end is 1 ½" from the top seam, and the outside edge of the handle is 1 ¾" from the side seam. Use a removable ink pen to mark where the hande should be positioned. Following the manufacturer's directions, stitch the handles to the bag. Note: If your handle is a different style, use these measurements as a guide.

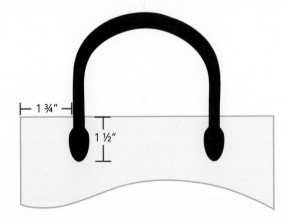

11 Sew the bottom edge of the lining closed and insert the lining into the bag, leaving just a bit of the lining showing around the top edge of the bag. Give the bag a final press.

Doll Mattress and Pillow

Doll Mattress and Pillow

This doll bedding set is a perfect fit for the Ikea wooden doll bed, but it can be used on its own as well. The perfect little accessory for the perfect little bed... goldilocks would definitely approve!

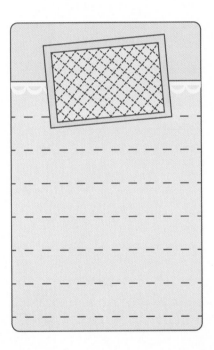

HELPFUL TIP

To adjust the mattress to fit another bed size, simply measure your bed for the desired width and height then add 1 ½" to each of these measurements and proceed from step 5. Following the instructions given, this will always result in a mattress that is approximately 1" thick. (For example if your doll bed accommodates a 5" x 7" mattress, follow steps 1-3 using large enough cuts of fabric so that your total unfinished top and bottom pieces measure 6 ½" x 8 ½" at step 5).

MATTRESS SIZE	PILLOW SIZE
12" x 19" x 1"	10 ½ " x 6 ½"

» ½ yard linen

» FQ of contrast print fabric

» 14" length of lace or similar trim

» FQ quilt batting

» Polyester stuffing

····························· CUTTING ·····························

» **From contrast print**

One 13 ½" x 5" rectangle

» **From linen**

Two 13 ½" x 16" rectangles

One 13 ½" x 5" rectangle

» **From batting**

One 14" x 21" rectangle

····························· INSTRUCTIONS ·····························

1 To make the mattress top, lay the lace trim along one short side of a 13 ½" x 16" linen rectangle. Pin or glue-baste and sew in place. Then with right sides together, lay the contrast print along the lace edge and sew the two pieces together. Press the the seam allowance towards the contrast print.

 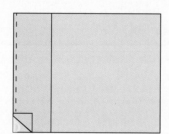 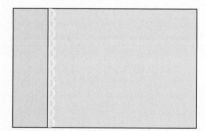

2 Spray or pin baste the batting to the wrong side of the pieced top and quilt as desired.

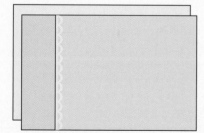 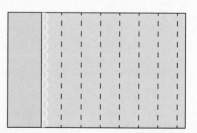

3 To make the mattress bottom, sew the two remaining linen pieces together, leaving a 4" opening at center (for turning). Make sure to backstitch at both ends of the opening. Press seam open.

4" opening

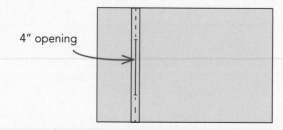

4 Pin and sew the quilted mattress top and bottom right sides together. Trim to measure 13 ½" x 20 ½". Cut out a ½" square from each corner.

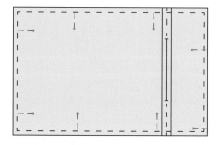

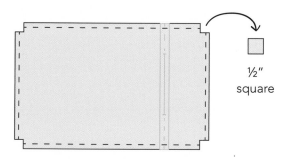

½"
square

5 To shape the mattress, fold one corner right sides together, aligning the side seams. Pin the seams in opposite directions so the quilt batting layers nest against each other, and sew across the raw edges with a ¼" seam. Repeat for all corners.

6 Turn the mattress right side out, and gently ease out the corners. Fill loosely with polyfill. It should not be puffy in the middle. It looks best when filled uniformly even, so it looks like a mattress. Hand-stitch the opening closed.

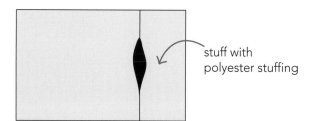

stuff with polyester stuffing

» 1 F8 fabric for front

» 1 F8 fabric for back

» 1/16 yard contrast fabric for binding

» 1 F8 quilt batting

» Polyester stuffing

CUTTING

» *From Front F8*
One 11" x 7" rectangle

» *From Back F8*
One 7 ½" x 7" rectangle
One 3 ½" x 7" rectangle

» *From Binding Fabric*
One 2" x WOF strip

» *From Quilt Batting*
One 11" x 7" rectangle

INSTRUCTIONS

1 To make the pillow front, lay the front piece onto the batting. Pin or spray baste the layers together and quilt as desired. Trim to measure 10 ½" x 6 ½".

 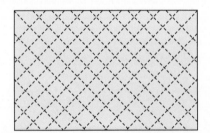

2 To make the pillow back, lay the two back pieces right sides together, aligning them along the 6 ½" side. Sew the pieces together, but leave a 4" opening. Reinforce the ends of the seams at the opening. Press seam open.

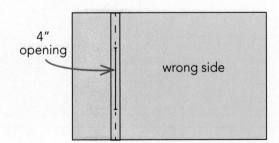

4" opening

wrong side

3 With wrong sides together, pin and sew the front and the backd back pieces together. Bind the edges.

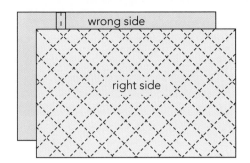

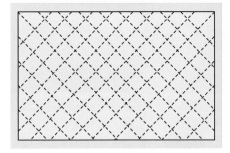

4 Stuff gently and loosley with polyester batting. Then hand-stitch the back opening closed.

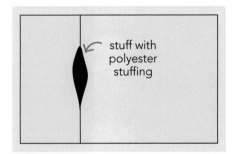

Doll Quilt

This doll quilt was made to go perfectly hand in hand with the doll bed mattress and pillow, but of course, you don't need either of those to make a doll quilt. And if your daughters are like mine, the more doll quilts the better! I love how this looks with its side borders draping over the sides of your favorite dolly.
I also love that this is for sure an afternoon make, so if someone needs a new doll quilt stat- no problem! It'll be ready to keep any little friends warm in a just a few hours.

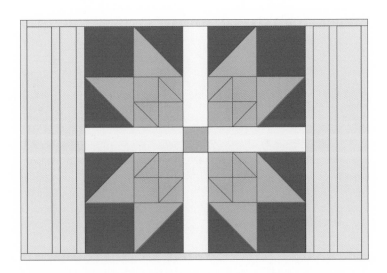

SIZE
21" x 14"

» 4 FQs of assorted fabrics (green, pink, red, and blue)

» 1 F8 of white fabric

» ½ yard backing

» ¼ yard inner border/binding

» 23" x 15" quilt batting

» *From Green FQ*

(A) Four 2 ½" squares

(B) Five 2" squares

» *From Pink Fq*

(C) Four 2" squares

(D) Four 2 ½" squares

(E) Four 4 ⅛" squares

» *From Red Fq*

(F) Four 4 ⅛" squares

(G) Four 3 ½" squares

» *From White F8*

(H) Four 6 ½" x 2 " rectangles

» *From Inner Border/Binding ¼ Yard*

(I) Four 14" x 1" strips

Two 2" x WOF strips (binding)

» *From blue FQ*

(J)Two 14" x 1 ½" strips

(K)Two 14" x 2" strips

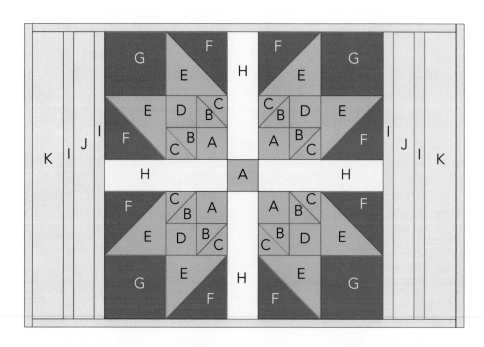

1   Pair up one B and one C square. Lay them right sides together. Draw a diagonal line on the backside of one square. Sew ¼" to either side of the drawn line. Cut along the drawn line. Press each seam open. Trim the half-square triangle (HST) to measure 2" . Make 8 of these HSTs.

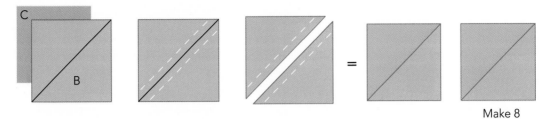

Make 8

2   Lay out two HSTs, one A square and one D square as shown. Sew them together and press seams open. Make 4 of these units

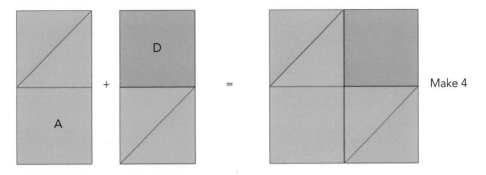

Make 4

3   Repeat step 1 with the E and F squares, trimming them to measure 3 ½".

Make 8

4   Repeat step 2 with a unit from step 2, 2 HSTs from step 3, and one G square. Make 4 of these units.

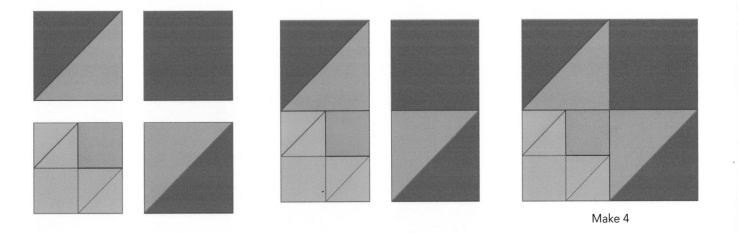

Make 4

5 Sew the 4 pieced units from step 4, the H strips, and the remaining A square together as shown. Press towards the white. The pieced unit should measure 14" square.

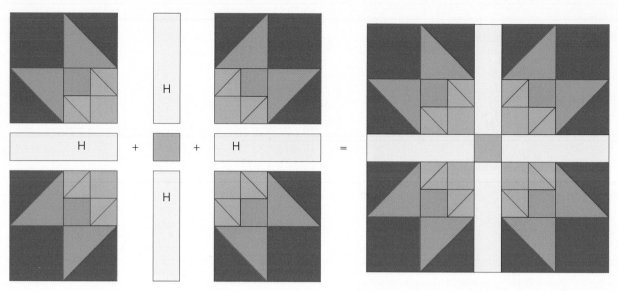

6 To make one pieced border, sew together two I strips, one J stirps, and one K strip together as shown. Press seams open. Repeat to make the othe pieced border. Sew the borders to the sides of the pieced center.

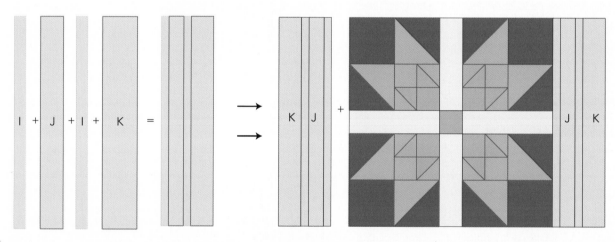

7 Your quilt top is now finished. Place the backing fabric right side down (wrong side up). Place the batting on top of it. Place the quilt top on top of batting, right side up. Spray or pin baste together. Quilt as desired and bind using your preferred method.

Chloe Cat

Chloe Cat has the finest whiskers in town and she is quite proud of them. She and Plum Mouse are best friends, and they share everything from tea to cheese and clothes! So similar are they, apart from the heads on their shoulders, Chloe and Plum have found only one thing different about themselves: Chloe's legs are a wee bit longer. And Chloe always wears socks. Stripey socks are her favorite!

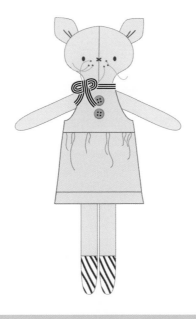

SIZE
4" x 14"

For Cat

» FQ linen for body

» 1 charm square contrast for socks

» 2 charm squares pink/peach for inner ears

» Card stock or cereal box for making templates

» 1 skein brown (3799 DMC) floss for face embroidery

» White waxed, upholstery, or regular thread for whiskers

» Polyester stuffing

» Fabric marker, like a FriXion pen

» Hemostats (surgical tool), bamboo skewer, or pencil to stuff limbs

For Dress

» 1 F8 fabric for dress

» 2 small buttons for dress

» From body fabric
Four heads with the template (cut two reversed)
Two ears with the template
Two bodies with the template
Eight strips 1 ½" x 4 ½" for arms and legs

» From socks fabric
Four strips 1 ½" x 3"

» From ear lining fabric
Two ears with the template

» From dress fabric
Two bodices (one outside, one lining) with the template
One skirt rectangle 20" x 4 ½"

1 To make an ear, pin and sew the body and inner ear pieces together, leaving the bottom edge open. Clip the fabric seam allowance and turn right side out. Press gently. Fold a small pleat in the center of the straight edge. Pin the pleat, and secure it with a scant ¼" seam. With the sewing machine, stitch over the gathers to secure them in place. Make the second ear.

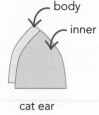

body
inner

cat ear

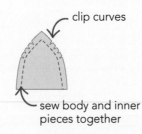

clip curves

sew body and inner
pieces together

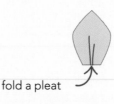

fold a pleat

sew to
secure pleat

2 To make the head front, pin and sew both head front pieces right sides together along the center seam. Reinforce the bottom end of the seam. Gently clip and press the seam. Repeat to make the head back. To make the face, use the photograph as a guide to mark the eyes, nose, and whiskers on the head front. Embroider the features with 2 strands of floss using a satin stitch and french knots . Add each whisker with the white thread (waxy or upshosltery thread is stiffer, but if you can't find any, soft whiskers make with regular thread is still adorable).

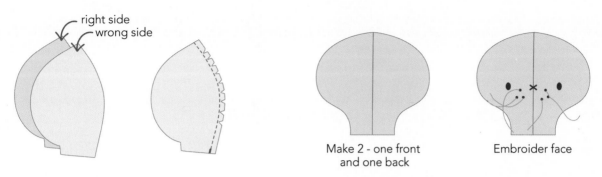

right side
wrong side

Make 2 - one front
and one back

Embroider face

3 To add the ears, pin one ear onto the head front, right sides together, and baste in place with a scant ¼" seam. Repeat to add the other ear. To form the head, pin the face and head back pieces right sides together - making sure the ears are tucked in - and sew around the head leaving the neck open. Reinforce both ends of the seam. Clip along the curved seam allowances, turn the head right side out and press gently. Stuff with polyester stuffing.

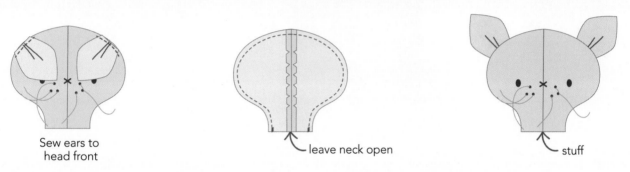

Sew ears to
head front

leave neck open

stuff

4 To make an arm, pin and sew two arm strips right sides together, sewing rounded corners at the bottom for the paw and leaving the opposite end open. Reinforce both ends of the seam. Gently trim and clip the rounded end. Turn the arm right side out and stuff gently as desired, leaving about ½" empty at the opening. Baste the opening closed to secure stuffing inside. Repeat for remaining limbs. For the legs, sew the sock strips to the bottom of the leg strips first, then follow the above instructions.

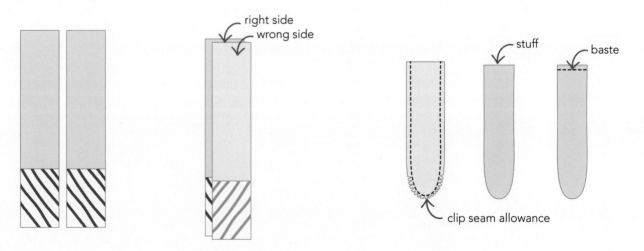

right side
wrong side

stuff

baste

clip seam allowance

5 Attaching the limbs is a bit fiddly so just take your time. Start with the legs. Pin and baste them to the body front with a scant ¼" seam. Lay the body back onto the legs and sew the front and back together with a partical seam as shown, securing the legs in place. Reinforce both ends of the seam.

6 Move the body back and legs out of the way to pin and baste one arm in place, angling it slightly towards the bottom of the body. Sew the body front and back together to secure that arm. Reinforce the seam at the neck. Repeat with the second arm (this is where it gets fiddly with all the limbs coming out the neck hole).

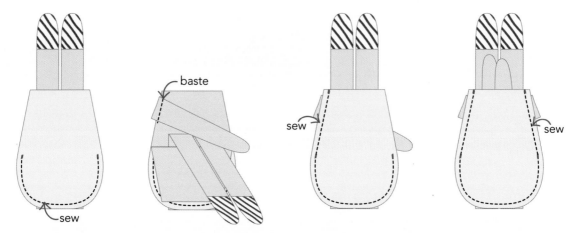

7 Turn the body right side out and stuff. Fold ½" of the neck opening into the body and hand baste in place. Insert the head into the body opening about ½". Pin the head in place and hand stitch neatly.

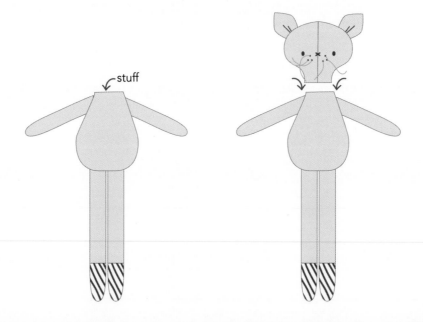

8 To make the cat dress, lay both bodice pieces right sides together. Starting and ending with reinforcing stitches, and sew along the top edge only as shown below, leaving the side and bottom edges open. Clip and trim the curved seam allowances. and top corners. Then fold and press the bottom edge of the lining piece wrong sides together by ¼".

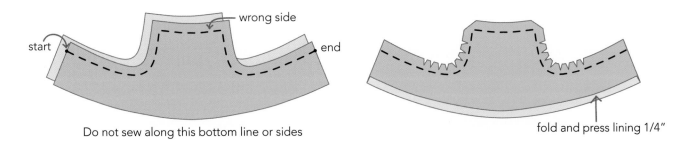

start

wrong side

end

Do not sew along this bottom line or sides

fold and press lining 1/4"

9 Turn the bodice right side out and press well. Set aside.

10 For the skirt part of the dress, fold ¼" twice along one 20" side of the skirt piece and press. Stitch the hem in place. Along the other 20" side, sew an row of basting stiches with a scant ¼". Pull the threads to make the gathered edge 8 ½" (or the length of the bottom edge of the bodice). Sew along the gathered stitches to secure them in place.

11 Pin the gathered edge of the skirt to the folded bottom edge of the bodice front, right sides together. It may be helpful to pin the bodice lining out of the way. Sew the skirt to the bodice with a ¼" seam. Align the folded edge of the bodice lining to the wrong side of the skirt and pin well. Sew the bodice to the skirt ⅛" from the folded edge. Now the raw gathered seam allowance is hidden between the bodice front and lining pieces.

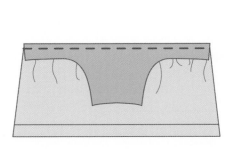

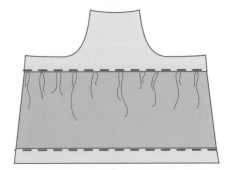

12 Fold the dress in half lengthwise wrong sides together and sew the back edges together with a ¼" seam. Trim the seam allowances with pinking shears and press open.

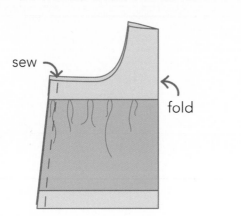
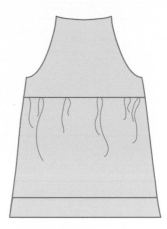

13 Cut an 18" length of ribbon. Center and align the top edge of the ribbon with the top edge of the bodice, right sides facing out. Hand or machine sew the ribbon to the bodice along the top edge. Then add two little buttons to the front of the bodice.

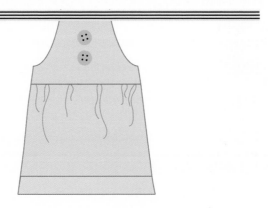

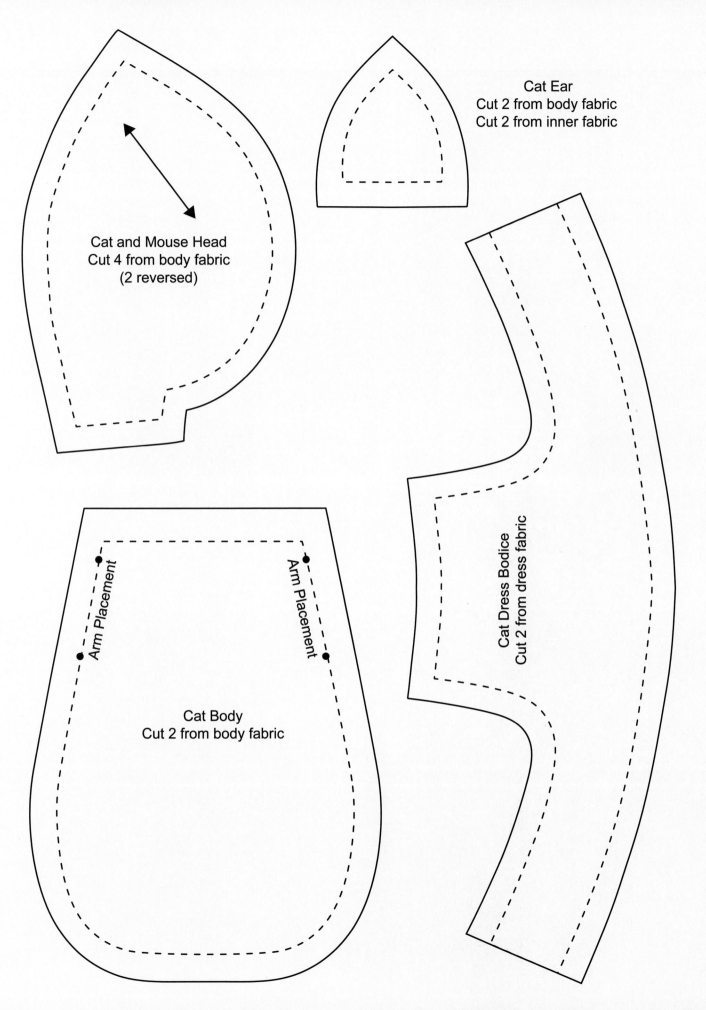

Cat and Mouse Head
Cut 4 from body fabric
(2 reversed)

Cat Ear
Cut 2 from body fabric
Cut 2 from inner fabric

Arm Placement

Arm Placement

Cat Body
Cut 2 from body fabric

Cat Dress Bodice
Cut 2 from dress fabric

Plum Mouse

Plum mouse likes jasmine tea and cheese with honey. She's a darling mouse that never causes any trouble and makes a wonderful addition to any home. Her dress is simple and works best in a finer fabric that has some drape, such as rayon, lawn, or voile- though any fabric will do. I'm sure she'd love a whole wardrobe of dresses, actually and as a well-mannered mouse she will sit patiently by while you sew them.

SIZE
4" x 10"

For Mouse

» FQ linen for body

» 2 charm squares pink/peach for inner ears

» 1 skein pink (818 DMC) floss for nose embroidery

» Cardstock or cereal box for making templates

» 1 skein brown (3799 DMC) floss for face embroidery

» White waxed, upholstery, or regular thread for whiskers

» Polyester stuffing

» Fabric marker, like a FriXion pen

» Hemostats (surgical tool), bamboo skewer, or pencil to stuff limbs

For Dress

» 1 F8 fabric for dress

» 30" length of lace or ribbon approx. ⅜" wide for dress

» *From Body Fabric*

Four heads with the template (cut two reversed)

Two ears with the template

Two bodies with the template

Four strips 1 ½" x 3" for arms and four strips 1 ½" x 3 ½" for legs

» *From Ear Lining Fabric*

Two ears with the template

» *From Dress Fabric*

Two dress panels (one front, one back) with the template

1 To make an ear, pin and sew the body and inner ear pieces together, leaving the bottom edge open. Clip the fabric seam allowance and turn right side out. Press gently. Fold a small pleat in the center of the straight edge. Pin the pleat, and secure it with a scant ¼" seam. With the sewing machine, stitch over the gathers to secure them in place. Make the second ear.

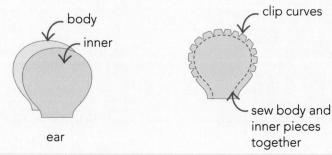

body
inner

ear

clip curves

sew body and
inner pieces
together

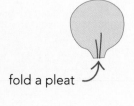

fold a pleat

sew to
secure pleat

2 To make the head front, pin and sew both head front pieces right sides together along the center seam. Reinforce the bottom end of the seam. Gently clip and press the seam. Repeat to make the head back. To make the face, use the photograph as a guide to mark the eyes, nose, and whiskers on the head front. Embroider the features with 2 strands of floss using a satin stitch and french knots . Add each whisker with the white thread (waxy or uphosltery thread is stiffer, but if you can't find any, soft whiskers make with regular thread is still adorable).

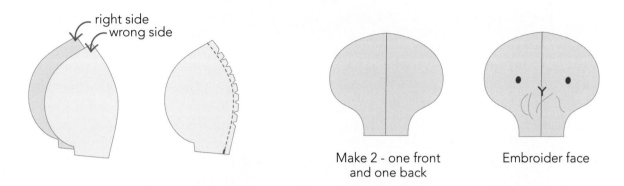

right side
wrong side

Make 2 - one front
and one back

Embroider face

3 To add the ears, pin one ear onto the head front, right sides together, and baste in place with a scant ¼" seam. Repeat to add the other ear. To form the head, pin the face and head back pieces right sides together - making sure the ears are tucked in - and sew around the head leaving the neck open. Reinforce both ends of the seam. Clip along the curved seam allowances, turn the head right side out and press gently. Stuff with polyester stuffing.

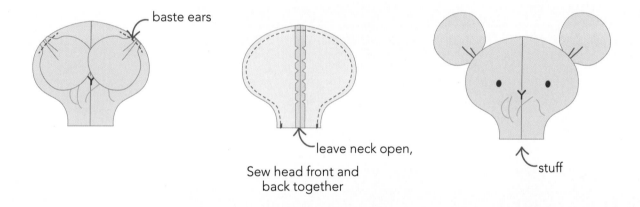

baste ears

leave neck open,

Sew head front and
back together

stuff

4 To make an arm, pin and sew two arm strips right sides together, sewing rounded corners at the bottom for the paw and leaving the opposite end open. Reinforce both ends of the seam. Gently trim and clip the rounded end. Turn the arm right side out and stuff gently as desired, leaving about ½" empty at the opening. Baste the opening closed to secure stuffing inside. Repeat for remaining limbs.

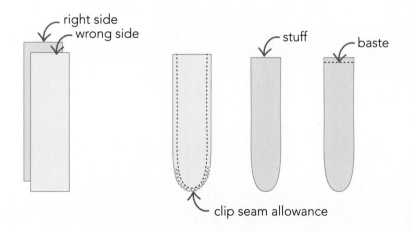

right side
wrong side

stuff

baste

clip seam allowance

5 Attaching the limbs is a bit fiddly so just take your time. Start with the legs. Pin and baste them to the body front with a scant ¼" seam. Lay the body back onto the legs and sew the front and back together with a partical seam as shown, securing the legs in place. Reinforce both ends of the seam.

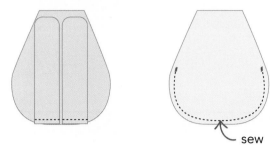

sew

6 Move the body back and legs out of the way to pin and baste one arm in place, angling it slightly towards the bottom of the body. Sew the body front and back together to secure that arm. Reinforce the seam at the neck. Repeat with the second arm (this is where it gets fiddly with all the limbs coming out the neck hole).

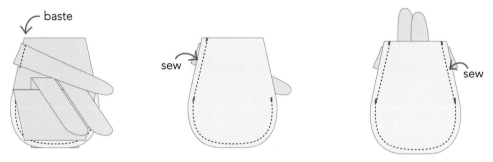

baste

sew

sew

7 Turn the body right side out and stuff. Fold ½" of the neck opening into the body and hand baste in place. Insert the head into the body opening about ½". Pin the head in place and hand stitch neatly.

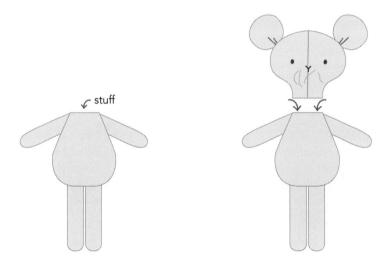

stuff

8 To make the mouse dress, fold and press each "armhole" edge ¼" twice towards the wrong side. Sew the hem close to the edge of the inner fold.

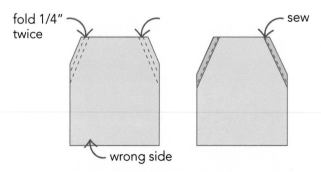

fold 1/4" twice

sew

wrong side

9 To make the neck, fold and press one ⅜" towards the wrong side, and then repeat with a scant ¼" fold. Sew the hem in place with a scant ¼" seam. These folds will form the casing for the lace or ribbon tie.

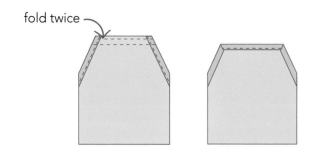

fold twice

10 Now lay the front and back pieces right sides together and sew the side seams. Zigzag the raw seam allowances and press open.

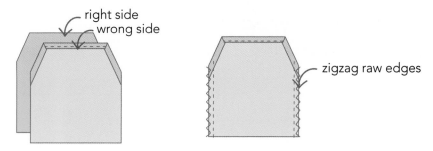

right side
wrong side

zigzag raw edges

11 Fold and press the bottom edge ¼" twice towards the inside of the dress. Sew the seam with a scant ¼". Cut a 10" length of lace and sew it around the bottom, trimming as necessary and folding the raw edges in for a neat finish.

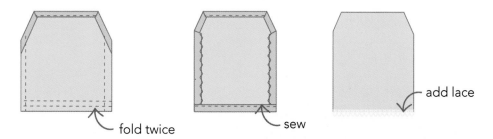

fold twice

sew

add lace

12 To finish the neck, loosely thread a 17" length of ribbon or lace though the casing front and back. Once the dress is on the mouse, cinch and tie the closure at the side of the neck.

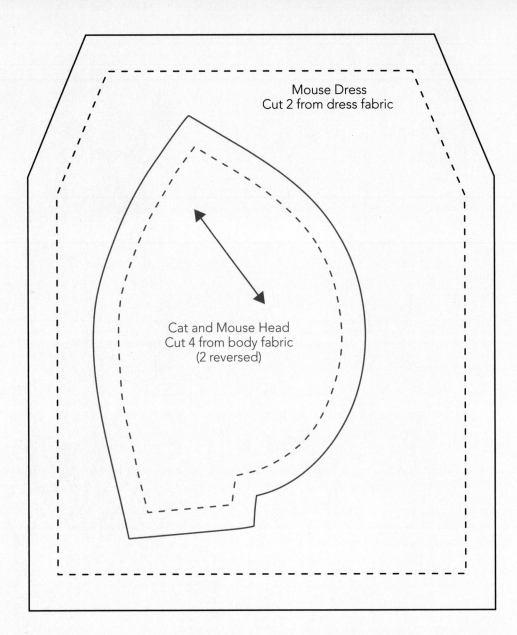

Mouse Dress
Cut 2 from dress fabric

Cat and Mouse Head
Cut 4 from body fabric
(2 reversed)

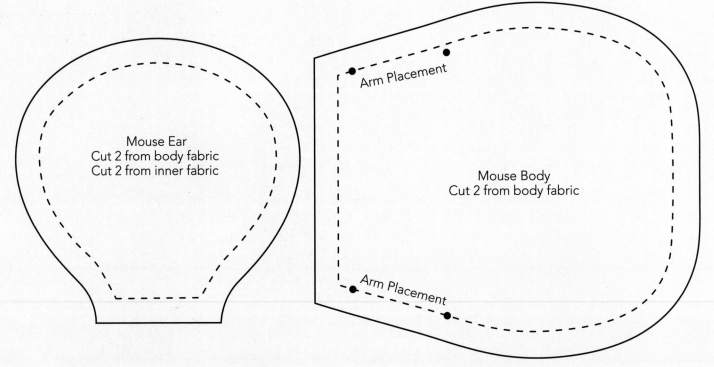

Mouse Ear
Cut 2 from body fabric
Cut 2 from inner fabric

Mouse Body
Cut 2 from body fabric

Arm Placement

Arm Placement

Thimble Basket

I like being organized. I like it even more when I have pretty storage to use. This sweet little basket does just that - keeps things together attractively. It's the perfect size to put lots of spools or other notions near your sewing machine. But it's also versatile enough to give to a darling little child for tiny collectibles. Not matter how you use it, this patchwork basket will quietly help keep your home organized, even if it's just in a small way.

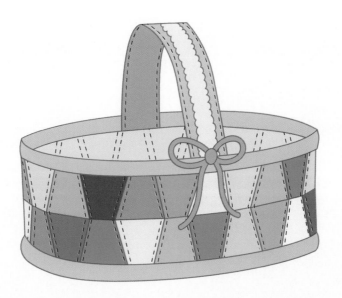

SIZE
4" x 7" x 2 ½"

» 44 squares of assorted cotton prints, 2 ½" for patchwork

» 1 Fat Quarter of cotton print for lining

» 1 Fat Quarter of contrast print for binding, handle, and bottom

» 1 Fat Quarter of cotton batting

» 1 length of double-edged lace 8" x ⅝" (approx.)

» 1 12" length of ribbon, ⅜" wide (approx.)

.... CUTTING ....

» *From Assorted Cotton Prints*
Forty four thimble shapes using template

» *From Lining*
One rectangle 2 ½" x 20 ½" for sides
One rectangle 6" x 10" bottom

» *From Contrast Print*
Two bias-cut strips 1 ¼" x 24" for single-fold binding
One bias-cut rectangle 3 ½" x 8 ½" for handle
One rectangle 6" x 10" for bottom

» *From Batting*
One rectangle 2 ½" x 20" for sides
One rectangle 6" x 10" for bottom
One rectangle 6" x 7 ½" for handle

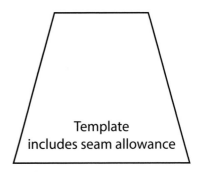

Template
includes seam allowance

.... INSTRUCTIONS ....

1 Sew the thimble shapes together into two rows of 22. Press seams open.

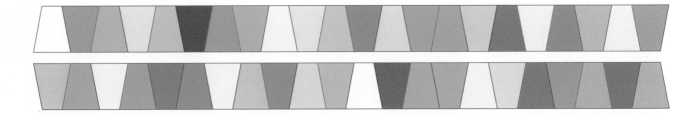

2 Join each row together at the ends to form a complete circle. With right sides together, join the two circular rows, matching up the seams to create the thimble pattern. Press seam open.

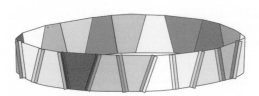
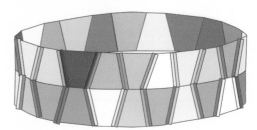

3 Turn the patchwork right side out. Pin the batting strip to the wrong side of the patchwork oval. (It may seem like the batting is too long, but it is not. Match the ends and then work the batting to fit smoothly.) Baste the two layers together around both the top and bottom edges with a scant ¼".

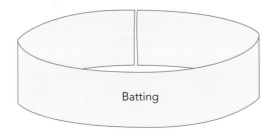

Batting

Batting

4 Sew the short ends of the lining strip together to form a complete circle. Press seam open. Insert with the wrong side of the lining against the batting. Baste around the both top and bottom edges with a scant ¼".

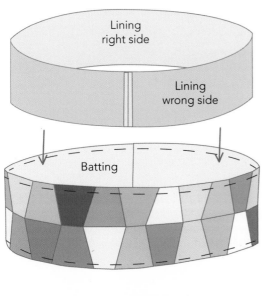

Lining
right side

Lining
wrong side

Batting

5 Quilt the 3 layers together as desired.

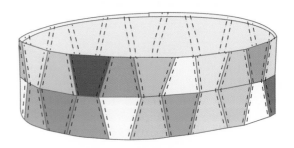

6 With right sides together, machine sew a binding strip to the outside top edge of the patchwork, but do not hand sew it to the inside yet.

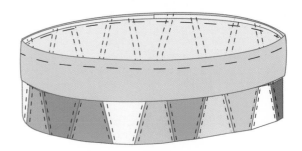

7 To make the basket bottom, layer the lining, batting, and contrast print rectangles, and quilt as desired. Use the oval template to cut out the bottom.

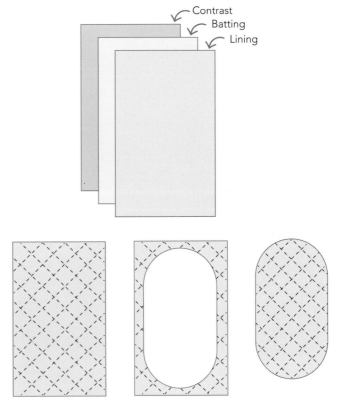

Contrast
Batting
Lining

8 Fold the bottom oval in half and mark the folds with pins. Open and refold in the opposite direction, mark the folds with pins. Use the same method to find the four center points for the patchwork and mark with pins. With wrong sides together, pin the patchwork to the bottom, matching the pins. With the patchwork facing up, sew the two pieces together.

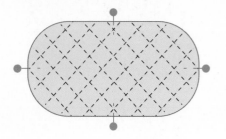 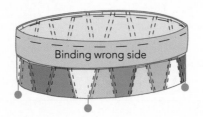 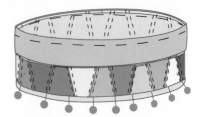

9 Bind the bottom edge with single-fold binding.

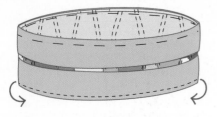 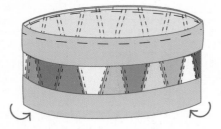 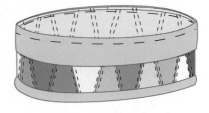

10 To make the handle, fold the handle fabric rectangle in half right sides together and press. Open, and lay the batting strip along the center line. Fold the top edge onto the batting and fold the bottom edge up an equal amount. Then align both folded edges. Pin and sew the folded edges together. Then sew a second row of top stitching along the other edge of the handle.

11 Machine or hand sew a length of lace down the center of the handle, if desired.

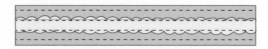

12 To attach the handle, pin one end to the center front of the basket, aligning the raw edges with wrong sides together. Baste with a scant ¼". Repeat with the other end of the handle to the center back of the basket.

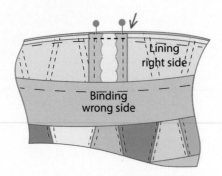

13 Hand-stitch the top binding to the lining of the basket. The binding will cover the raw handle edges.

14 To keep the handle standing up, fold it up and hand-stitch it to the top edge of the binding with a slip stitch. Then glue or stitch a ribbon bow to the end of the handle as a nice decorative final detail.

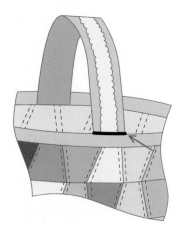

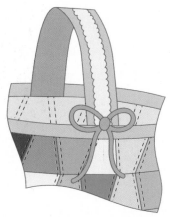

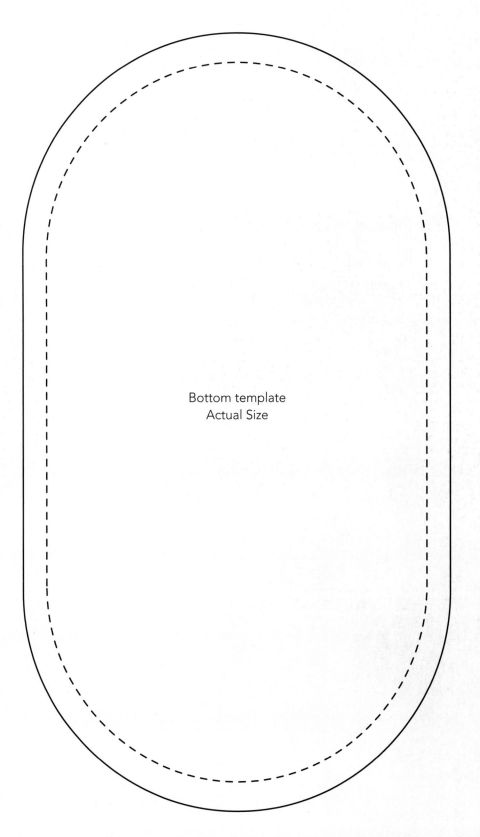

Bottom template
Actual Size

Bless You Tissue Box Cover

Saying "bless you" when someone sneezes is an old-fashioned tradition. But it's such a charming, not to mention polite, thing to say so I hope it never goes out of style. You only need a handful of scrap fabric and batting, and a bit of embroidery floss, to pretty up a utilitarian tissue box. Once you make one, I think you'll want to make several for all your favourite people. Oh, and of course the embroidery is completely optional. This project looks just as cute with pretty fabrics alone!

SIZE
4 ½" x 4 ½" x 5 "

» 1 tissue box 4 ½" x 4 ½" x 5"

» 7 charm squares of assorted cotton print

» 1 Fat Eighth of linen

» 1 Fat Eighth of fabric for lining

» ¼ yard or FQ cotton batting

» 1 skein dark brown embroidery floss (DMC 938)

» Embroidery hoop (optional)

» Embroidery needle

» Erasable fabric marker

bless you
Template

» *From 6 Of The Charm Squares (For Sides)*
Two rectangles 2" x 4" each for a total of 12 rectangles

» *From 1 Charm Square (For Single-Fold Binding)*
Two rectangles 1 ½" x 5"

» *From Linen*
Two rectangles 5" x 2 ½"
Two rectangles 5" x 4 ½"

» *From Lining*
One strip 18 ½" x 4 ½"

» *From Batting*
Two rectangles 4 ½" x 5 ½"
Two rectangles 4 ½" x 8"

1 To make one side panel, sew together 3 assorted prints and one 2 ½" x 5" linen rectangle. Press seams open. Embroider a running stitch on the linen ⅛" above the seam with 2 plies of floss. On the wrong side of this panel, center a 4" x 4 ½" batting rectangle. Pin or spray baste in place and quilt as desired. The panel should measure 5" x 5 ¾". Make 2 side panels.

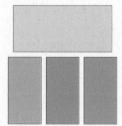 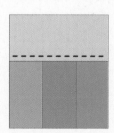   

2 To make the front panel, sew together 3 assorted prints and one 5" x 4 ½" linen rectangle. Press seams open. Trace the embroidery words onto the linen, and stitch with 2 plies of floss with a back stitch. Then add the running stitch, also with 2 plies. On the wrong side of this panel, center a 4 ½" x 8" batting rectangle, making sure to align the top edges. Pin or spray baste in place and quilt as desired. The panel should measure 5" x 8 ¼". Repeat to make the back panel (embroidered words are optional).

3 To sew a single-fold binding strip to the top edge of the front panel, lay a binding strip along the top edge, right sides together, and sew with a ¼" seam. Fold and press ¼" the other raw edge of the binding, wrong sides together. Fold the binding over the raw edges and sew the folded edge to the batting on the wrong side of the panel. Then embroider a running stitch ⅛" from the binding seam. Repeat for the back panel.

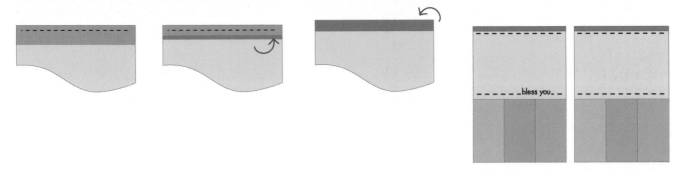

4 To assemble the cover, find the center of the top edge of one short side. With right sides together, align the binding edges to the center mark of the short panel as shown. Pin and sew the pieces together, starting and stopping at the ¼" point at both ends.

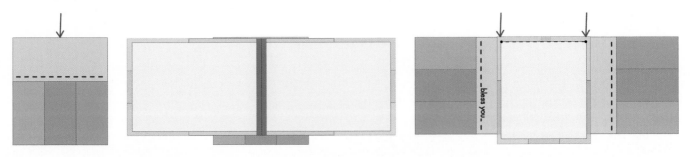

5 Clip the seam allowance on the long panels at the ¼" marks. Pivot one long panel at the clip to align the sides. Pin the sides together, taking care to match the embroidery stiching. Sew the side seam, starting at the ¼" mark where the top seam ends. Repeat for the remaining 3 sides.

6 Fold the lining strip in half, right sides together, and sew the short ends together. Press seam open.

7 With the tissue box cover right side out and the lining inside out, slide the lining over the tissue box cover, and pin them together around the bottom edges. Sew around the bottom edge. Fold the lining inside the cover and press along the seam. Turn the cover inside out. Fold the top edge of the lining under and hand stitch the fold to the batting inside.

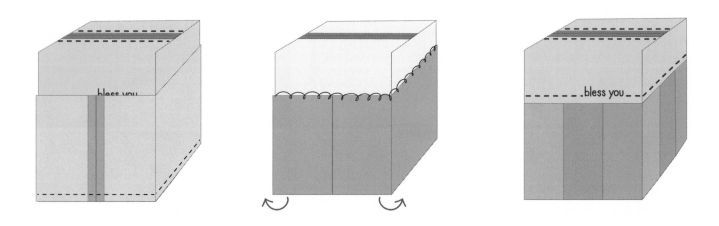

8 Turn the cover right side out and press all the seams to form a box shape. Insert the tissue box inside the cover.

Olivia Pencil Case

I have a thing for cute pencils. I think it started when I was little. One year Santa put a whole package of personalized pencils in my stocking. These pencils made a big impression on me because the unusual spelling of my first name meant that I would never find an "over-the-counter" personalized keychain or name plate. It appears that my thing for pencils has become a thing for pencil cases. It's pretty much my go-to gift for everyone from little children to teachers, to friends and family. They're so practical, and this pattern sews up super quick! I've used a cheater print to simulate patchwork, which makes the completion time that much faster. But you can just as easily make your own slab of piecing or applique to suit the recipient, and your creative mood.

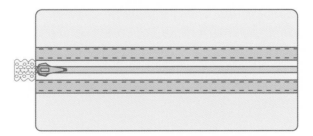

SIZE
2 ¾" x 8"

» 1 F8 of a cotton print (consider a cheater print!)

» 1 F8 of heavy interfacing

» 1 F8 fusible web

» 1 zipper, 8"

» 2" scrap of double-edged lace

» *From Cotton Print*
Two rectangles 5 ½" x 8 ½" (for body and lining)
Two strips 1 ½" x 8 ½" (for zipper binding)
Two rectangles 1 ½" x 2 ⅝" (for inner binding)

» *From Interfacing*
One rectangle 5 ½" x 8"

» *From Fusible Web*
Two rectangles 5 ½" x 8 ½"

1 To make the body, follow the manufacturer's instructions to adhere the body fabric rectangle to one side of the interfacing with one rectangle of fusible web rectangle, making sure the interfacing is centered (it is ¼" smaller on the short sides to reduce seam allowance bulk). Repeat with the lining fabric and remaining fusible web on the other side of the interfacing.

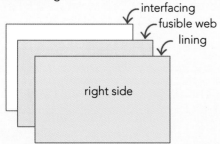
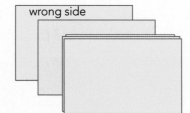

2 To add one zipper binding, pin a binding strip, right sides together, along an 8 ½" side of the body and sew with a generous ¼" seam. Make and press a ¼" fold along the raw edge of the binding strip wrong sides together. Then wrap the binding around the raw edge of the case onto the lining. Pin and sew along the first seam (in the ditch). Repeat with the other binding strip.

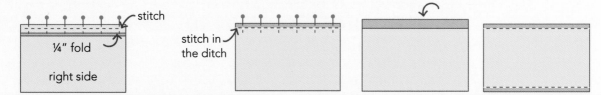

3 Install the zipper foot on your sewing machine. Lay the zipper right side up. Then lay one bound edge of the body, right side up, overlapping the zipper so the binding is about ⅛" away from the zipper teeth. Pin or just hold the zipper and body together, and sew along the outside edge of the binding. Sew a second row of top-stitching along the other binding edge.

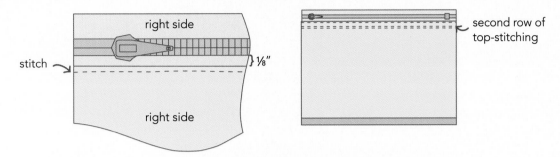

4 Open the zipper and repeat step 3 with the other sides of the zipper and body.

5 Fold the lace in half wrong sides together. Align the raw edges of the lace with the raw edge of the closed end of the zipper. Pin and baste in place with a scant ¼" seam.

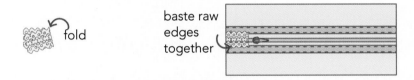

6 Turn the body inside out. Fold and pin the case in half with the zipper centered along the short ends. With the zipper half open, sew the ends closed. Be careful not to run over the metal parts of the zipper with the sewing machine needle.

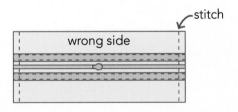

7 Repeat step 2 to bind the inside seam allowances with the 2 ⅝" strips.

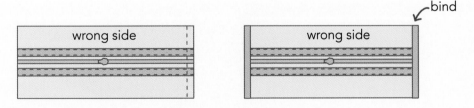

8 Turn the case right side out, shape the corners, and press the end seams.

Portfolio Tote

Portfolio Tote

When I needed a bag to hold drawing supplies for trips to the museum and botanical gardens, this bag was the perfect fit! The portfolio tote is simple, oversized in order to fit a large drawing pad, and has a single divider that adds extra support. Triangle patchwork on the front and back showcases a balance of sweet and modern fabrics.

SIZE
17 ½" x 13"

» 6 assorted F8s for triangle patchwork - DO NOT PREWASH

» FQ yd contrast fabric (linen) bag body

» ½ yd fabric for lining

» ⅓ yd fabric for divider

» 2" x WOF strip contrast fabric (stripe) for binding

» 42" of handle webbing

» ½ yd fusible fleece or quilt batting

» 1 FQ sturdy heavy weight pellon stabilizer for inside divider

» **Optional:** Leather scraps for patch and side tab, 42" of decorative cotton tape or ribbon (narrower than the handle webbing) for handle

» Fabric glue

» *From Each Of The Assorted F8s*
Two strips, 3" x 20". Sub-cut strips into 15 triangles for a total of 90 triangles.

» *From Contrast Body Fabric*
Four 18" x 3" rectangles

» *From Lining Fabric*
Two 18" x 13" rectangles

» *From Divider Fabric*
One 17 ½" x 23" rectangle

» *From Heavyweight Pellon Stabilizer*
One 17" x 10" rectangle

» *From Fusible Fleece Or Quilt Batting*
Two 19" x 14" rectangles for body
Two 15 ½" x 10" rectangles for divider

» *From Binding Fabric*
One 2" x 35" strip

» *From Handle Webbing*
Two lengths, 21"

» *From Decorative Ribbon Or Cotton Tape*
Two lengths, 21"

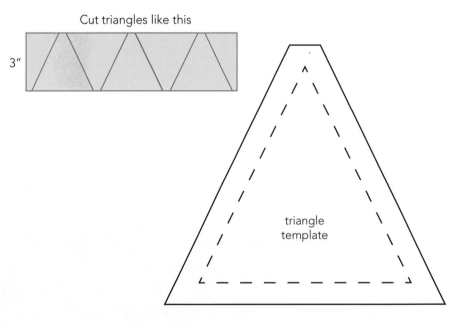

Cut triangles like this

3"

triangle template

1 To make the bag front, sew 45 triangles into 3 rows of 15 triangles each. Press all seams open. Trim the patchwork panel to measure 18" x 8". Then sew a contrast body rectangle to the bottom of the panel. Press seam towards the bottom.

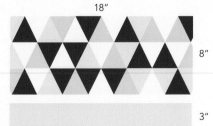

18"

8"

3"

2 Optional: To decorate the handle, apply fabric glue to the wrong side of a 21" length of decorative ribbon or cotton tape. With the glued side down, place the decoration along the center of the handle. Sew both sides of the tape in place. Repeat for the second handle.

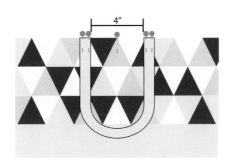

3 To add the handle to the bag front, find the center of the patchwork and mark with a pin. Aligning the raw edges of the handle, with the top edge of the patchwork and right sides together, pin the ends of the handle so the inside edges are 4" apart. Baste the handle ends to the patchwork with a scant ¼". Then sew another contrast body rectangle to the top edge of the bag front. Press seam towards the top.

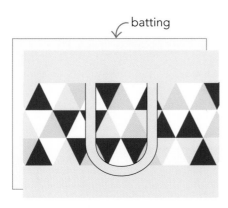

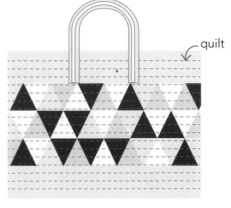

4 Layer the bag front and one 19" x 14" batting rectangle. Fuse or pin the layers together and quilt as desired. Trim the excess batting from around the edges.

5 Repeat steps 1 - 4 to make the back panel.

6 **Optional:** Add a leather/cotton patch to the center of the front panel, and/or a leather tab to the side seam.

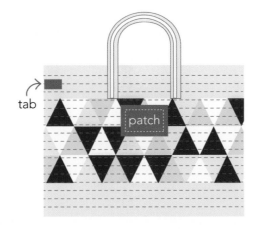

7 To form the bag, lay the body front and back pieces right sides together. Pin and sew the sides and bottom edges, and add a few reinforcing stitches at both ends of the seam. Clip the bottom corner seam allowances, press seams open and turn bag right side out. Press seams again.

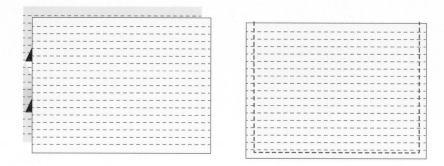

8 To make the center divider, fuse two pieces of fusible fleece to either side of the heavy weight Pellon stabilizer. Then press the divider fabric in half, wrong sides together.

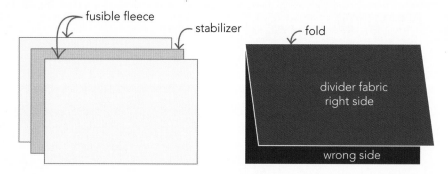

9 Center the stabilizer unit inside the divider fabric, snug to the top fold. Pin the bottom and top edges of the divider fabric to keep the stabilizer in place while quilting. Quilt ½" from top edge, then ¾" from the top edge, and then quilt rows 2" apart for the rest of the divider. Trim to measure 18" x 10 ½". The stabilizer should be at least ½" away from the bottom and side edges.

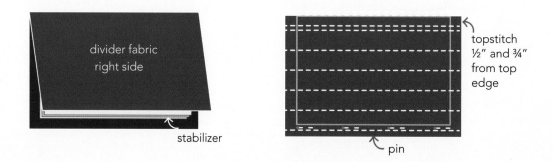

10 Layer the two lining rectangles and the stabilizer right sides together, aligning the bottom edges. Pin and sew along the sides and bottom edges with a ¼" seam. Press side seams open.

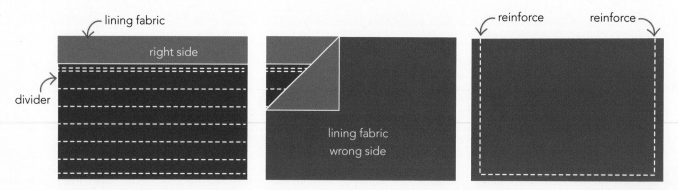

11 Insert the lining/divider unit inside the bag, matching the side seams. Pin and baste around the top edge with a scant ¼" seam.

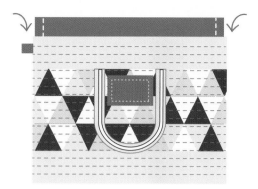

12 To make the binding for the top edge, press the binding strip in half lengthwise, wrong sides together. Open the short ends and sew them right sides together with a ¼" seam. Press seam open and refold/press the binding strip.

center seam

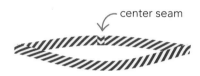

13 To attach the binding, fit it over the top of the bag, with right sides together, aligning the raw edges, and position the binding seam on the back side. Pin and sew the binding around the bag with a ¼" seam. Press the binding up, then fold the binding into the bag to cover the raw edges. Hand or machine sew the folded edge of the binding to the lining.

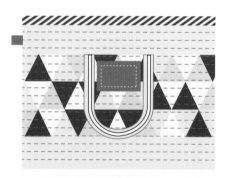

ACKNOWLEDGMENTS

Amy and Kristyne are so thankful for the opportunity to write this book and share their love of sewing 'pretty little things'. With gratitude they would like to mention the following people for their invaluable assistance along the way:

Kader and Ayhan Demirpehlivan of Tuva Publishing

Samantha Zulliger, the feedsack hunter extraordinary and generous friend
Nick Sinibaldi for unwavering support and for always having the right opinion
Lauren Schultz for endless words of encouragement

John Czepuryk for indulging my creative spirit, and for knowing how to cook
Anna Mae and Holly for always making the perfect cup of tea

Sewing with the best high quality fabrics and products makes an appreciable difference during the creative process. From fabrics to threads to embroidery floss to light tables to interfacing and stabilizer, Amy and Kristyne are grateful to the following companies for their contributions to the making of this book:

Andover Fabrics
Art Gallery Fabrics
Aurifil thread
Birch Fabrics
Dashwood Studios
DMC USA
Elea Lutz
Kaufman Fabrics
Lecien Fabrics
Moda Fabrics
Olfa
Pellon
Soak Wash Inc.
Sunny Day Supply
The Daylight Company
Windham Fabrics